ATLAS OF COLORADO

COLORADO LOCATION MAP

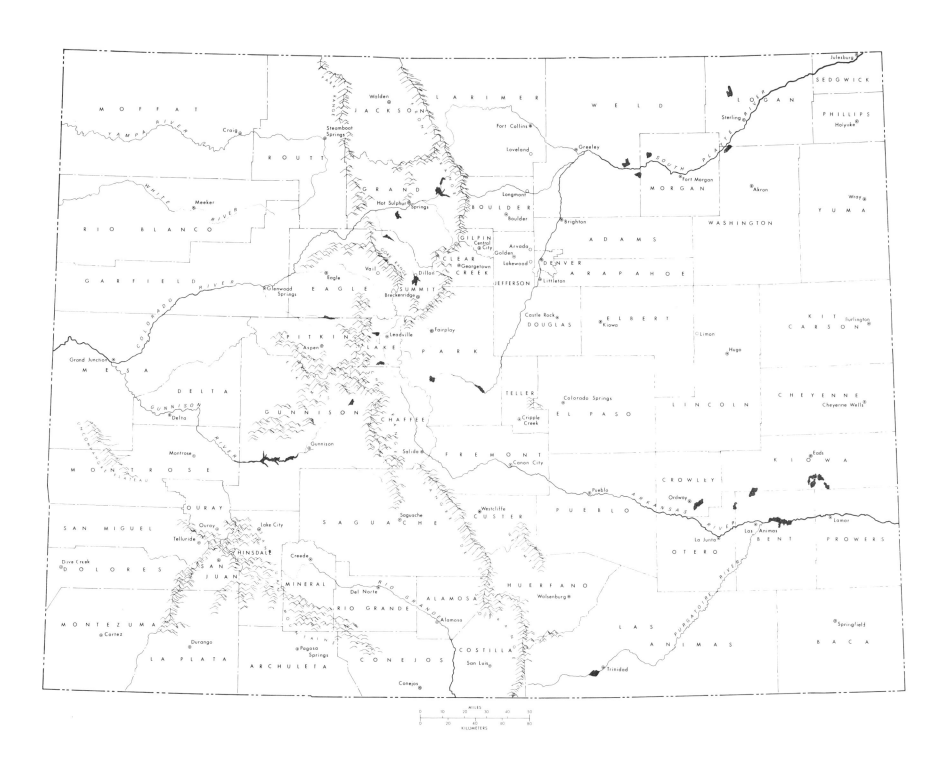

ATLAS
OF COLORADO

BY

KENNETH A. ERICKSON AND ALBERT W. SMITH

Research Assistants	*Graphic Artists*	*Production Assistants*
STAFFORD BINDER	KATHRYN INGRAHAM	RICHARD HEEDE
KATHRYN INGRAHAM	MARK LOEB	PATTI JOHNSON
JENNIFER NASH	GRANT MORRISON	DIANE LORENZ
	JENNIFER NASH	KRIS MATHISEN

Typing

CAROL WATSON

COLORADO ASSOCIATED UNIVERSITY PRESS

Copyright © 1985 by Colorado Associated University Press
Boulder, Colorado 80309
International Standard Book Numbers 0-87081-142-8 (cloth)
and 0-87081-143-6 (paper)
Library of Congress Catalog Card Number 84-072803
Printed in the United States of America
Designed by Bruce Campbell

Colorado Associated University Press is a cooperative publishing
enterprise supported in part by Adams State College, Colorado
State University, Fort Lewis College, Mesa College, Metropolitan
State College, University of Colorado, University of Northern
Colorado, University of Southern Colorado, and Western State College.

Contents

Preface and Acknowledgments

LARGE PROJECTS ORIGINATE in some early and diverse increments of words, ideas, proposals and, commonly, sputtering activity. As far back as the late 1950s, members of the Department of Geography, University of Colorado, had seen the need for and urged the development of a thematic atlas of the state. The key word was "thematic," to differentiate it from standard location maps of rivers, highways, towns, and political boundaries. Interest in the project remained alive, though languishing, for the next twenty years until the Colorado Associated University Press forced the issue with an offer of support and a request for a detailed proposal.

The guiding criteria for this atlas — other than the normal requisite of scientific accuracy — have been to provide a geographic appraisal, in cartographic form, of the social and physical elements, change, problems, and landscapes of the state for the general public in a concise, inexpensive manner. Talented students comprised most of the production staff; data, except for census information, were derived from local sources; execution of the maps depended greatly on screening one color with black to achieve distinctive patterns; and a small format compressed statewide maps to a modest but readable size.

The base map developed for the *Atlas of Colorado* is an original computation of Albers Conic Projection based on two standard parallels at 37°40'N and 40°20'N and centered on the meridian of 105°30'W. At an initial scale of 1:1,250,000 a graticule of 15' produced a finely textured, areally accurate plotting base.

The repeated theme of this atlas concerns the contrasts of three great physiographic provinces that Colorado's rectangular outline overrides. The Great Plains, the successive home of plains Indians, cowboys, and farmers, a landscape of grass and low relief, stretches from Texas to Alberta, Canada. The Rocky Mountains, a stringy, rough-textured fabric of intensely folded and glaciated highlands from New Mexico to British Columbia, attracts tourists and recreationists from throughout North America. The Colorado Plateau, identified with the American Southwest, encompasses a region of sharply contrasting landscapes: juniper-covered plateaus, arid valleys, small towns, and vast empty areas.

Colorado is all of these things.

In the production of this atlas we have relied heavily on the time, generosity, and information of many individuals and agencies whose contributions deserve mention.

First, without the seed money to cover initial material and production costs, the project could not have moved forward. Generous grants from the Frost Foundation of Denver, the Chancellor's discretionary fund of the University of Colorado, Mr. Malcolm S. Forbes, and the Vanetta Rickards Betts Memorial Fund have made a dream a reality. The University of Colorado has made contributions in other ways; particularly, the Department of Geography, which provided space and production facilities; the staff of the Western History Collection at Norlin Library; and individuals of the general faculty: William Bradley (Geology), Jack D. Ives (Mountain Geoecology), M. John Loeffler (Geography), John D. Marr (Biology), and Omer Stewart (Anthropology), whose commentaries added substantially to the text. Reviewers of the initial proposal provided sound advice and criticisms: R. L. Lehrer and Steven L. Scott of the University of Northern Colorado, Glen D. Weaver representing Colorado State University, and Louis F. Campbell, State Cartographer. Governmental personnel aided our research on several levels. At the federal level, Pat Rodrigues (Bureau of the Census) and Bob Alexander (U.S. Geological Survey) provided critical data. State information came from Hal Haney, Office of Tourism; Bruce Kenney, Rail Planning Office; Jon Scherschligt, Water Quality Control Division; David N. Wetzel, Colorado Historical Society; and Jo Ann Keith, Department of Education. Richard Veazey, Airport Engineering and Planning, and Lorena Donohue, Littleton Historical Society, gave freely of their time and knowledge. Staff people from the Clerk's Office, Colorado Supreme Court, the Weld County Extension Office, and the State Department of Highways provided hard-to-get data. Finally, for specific technical advice Robert Stoker, March Press, Inc.; Dr. Bruce Rippeteau, vice-president, Powers Elevation; Mike Lewis, Cooperative Extension Service, C.S.U.; and Frank Ugolini, Heritage Conservation and Recreation Service, merit special thanks.

Whatever credits emanate from this project must be shared with all those above; but whatever errors appear must rest solely with those below.

Kenneth A. Erickson
Albert W. Smith

ATLAS OF COLORADO

Territorial Evolution

O F ALL THE FIFTY states, only three, Colorado and neighboring Utah and Wyoming, have no natural boundaries. The limits of these states are arbitrarily selected parallels and meridians, true East–West and North–South lines respectively. As parts of the Earth's coordinate system (geographic grid), they form arcuate rectangles that are usually transformed into quadrangles when portrayed on flat maps. Accordingly in this atlas, Colorado is portrayed not as a perfect rectangle but rather as an area bounded by curving parallels and converging meridians.[1]

This arbitrary, mathematical designation of Colorado's borders is a relatively recent event in a complex evolution of successive claims and jurisdictions that spanned more than four centuries. Six nations — Spain, England, France, Mexico, Texas and the United States — have claimed all or parts of the state.

Early claims to Colorado territory were extensive and conflicting, with the French contesting strong Spanish claims that were based on discovery and widespread exploration. The Treaty of 1763 between Great Britain, France, and Spain partially resolved the issue of contested lands by eliminating the French from the North American mainland and restricting British jurisdiction to east of the Mississippi River. Colorado became undisputed Spanish soil until 1800 when at the Treaty of St. Ildefonso Napoleon purchased Louisiana (western Mississippi drainage) from Spain. Three years later he sold it to the United States for $15 million. Unfortunately, the southern and western boundaries were not defined in the earlier transfer from Spain to France. These contested boundaries were adjudicated in the Treaty of 1819 when that portion of Colorado south of the Arkansas River and west of the meridian extending northward from its headwaters was recognized as Spanish Territory.

During the next four decades (1819–1861), a rapid succession of events repeatedly changed the map of the region that was to become Colorado. First, Mexico gained independence and assumed control of Spain's northern territories in 1821. Second, Texas declared its independence from Mexico in 1836 and claimed the land between the Arkansas River and the Rio Grande, including an elongated panhandle bounded by meridians that extended northward from their headwaters to the 42nd parallel. Third, in 1845 Texas was admitted as a state whose boundaries included the disputed panhandle. (In reality Mexico had retained *de facto* ownership and control.) Fourth, after the Mexican-American War at the Treaty of Guadalupe-Hidalgo in 1848, Mexico ceded all possessions north of the Rio Grande and Gila River. With this cession, the area that now comprises the state of Colorado was finally and completely U.S. property.

In 1850, Texas relinquished her claim on the panhandle and other western lands for an award of $10 million, accepting the 36°30′ parallel as her northern (also present) boundary. Two new territories were organized: Utah to the west of the Continental Divide and New Mexico to the east of the Divide. The remainder of the Eastern Slope, variously defined as District of Louisiana, Missouri Territory, Indian Territory, or Unorganized Territory since its purchase from France, was subdivided in 1854 to create Nebraska Territory and Kansas Territory, separated by the 40th parallel. From parts of the four territories, Colorado was organized as a territory on February 28, 1861.

The mathematical boundaries established for the territory and later for the state contrast markedly with natural borders frequently selected to separate many claims and jurisdictions from c. 1700 to 1861. The Continental Divide and Front Range separated early Spanish and French claims, Spanish and American jurisdictions, and U.S. territories. The south bank of the Arkansas River figured repeatedly as the international border between the United States and Spain, Mexico, or Texas. The north bank of the Rio Grande formed a contested boundary between Mexico and the Republic of Texas. The Continental Divide still serves as a political boundary, but now on a local scale, for more than a score of counties. The two major rivers, on the other hand, currently serve as boundaries for only four counties, two in each drainage.

Surveyors completed the final chapter in the evolution of the state's boundaries. Working under the adverse physical and technical conditions of the nineteenth century, rather remarkable accuracy was attained in the field. With two exceptions, survey lines and their monuments varied only slightly from the designated parallels and meridians. Subsequent investigations have revealed two gross errors (by geodetic standards) in alignment that distort the mathematical symmetry of the state. The most obvious is a jog or offset of nearly one-half mile along the southern border in the vicinity of Edith. A less noticeable deviation was uncovered in a retracing of the western boundary in 1885. A divergence of more than 7° from the meridinal boundary that R. J. Reeves had surveyed across canyons and escarpments creates a westward bulge. To the layman these miscalculations are insignificant and are portrayed in this atlas only by exaggeration on the small-scale maps.

The eastern and western boundaries were originally designated as the 25th and 32nd meridians from Washington, D.C., but with the acceptance of Greenwich, England as the site of the prime meridian, the borders had to be readjusted. Since Greenwich lies 70°03′02″ east of Washington, the borders now have an awkward numbering. Most Coloradans, however, ignore the 3′ and 2″ (about 2.3 miles) noting that their state spans 7° of longitude between the 102nd and 109th meridians. No such "rounding" is needed latitudinally because parallels were always determined from the equator, 37° and 41° for the south and north borders, thus making the Centennial State a neat, compact, 4° × 7° quadrangle covering 104,247 square miles.

---

[1]An Albers Equal Area Projection was computed especially for the base maps of Colorado with 105½° West Longitude as the central meridian and 40°20′ and 37°40′ North Latitude as standard parallels.

Treaty of 1763

SPAIN

Treaty of St. Ildefonso 1800

SPAIN | FRANCE

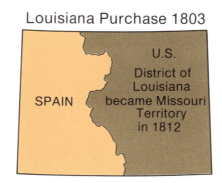

Louisiana Purchase 1803

SPAIN | U.S. District of Louisiana became Missouri Territory in 1812

Treaty with Spain 1819

SPAIN | Missouri Territory

Arkansas R.

Mexican Independence 1821

MEXICO | Missouri Territory

Texas Independence 1836

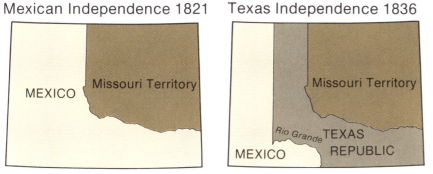

Missouri Territory

Rio Grande | TEXAS REPUBLIC

MEXICO

Texas Statehood 1845

Missouri Territory

MEXICO | TEXAS

Mexican Cession 1848

Missouri Territory

U.S. | Texas

U.S Territories 1850

Utah | Missouri

New Mexico

U.S. Territories 1854

Nebraska

Utah | Kansas

New Mexico

State of Colorado 1876

North and South Boundaries closely match the 37th and 41st parallels. East and West Boundaries lie 2 to 3 miles west of the 102nd and 109th Greenwich meridians respectively.

Colorado Territory 1861

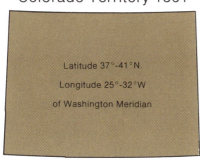

Latitude 37°-41°N.

Longitude 25°-32°W of Washington Meridian

	SPAIN
	FRANCE
	UNITED STATES
	MEXICO
	TEXAS

COLORADO BOUNDARIES
1800 to 1876

Landforms

GENERALLY RECOGNIZED AS the "Roof of the U.S.A.," Colorado is the epitome of geomorphic splendor and diversity. Its splendor is immortalized in the lyrics of *America the Beautiful,* composed by Katherine Lee Bates in the summer of 1893 after returning from her first trip to the summit of Pikes Peak. The opening lines capture the awesomeness, tranquility, and grandeur of the Rocky Mountain Front Range where 14,000-foot glaciated peaks rise majestically over irrigated valleys and productive plains. Diversity, too, is apparent. Within Colorado, all major relief features — mountains, plains, and plateaus — and all rock classes — igneous, sedimentary, and metamorphic — are conspicuously represented. Additionally, each relief unit is comprised of a myriad of small landforms that provide textural detail, and each rock class contains a multitude of rock types and minerals, many of which are economically significant.

To bring a sense of order and clarity to this terrestrial complexity, physical geographers and geologists create geomorphic regions. Ideally, these units have a distinctive surface (*terrain expression*) that is somewhat related to the character of the underlying bedrock (*geologic structure*). In Colorado, three such regions — the Southern Rockies, the Western Plateaus, and the High Plains — are recognized, each with its own distinctive elements of altitude, relief, and landforms.

The Mountains: The Southern Rockies, situated primarily in Colorado, make up a portion of a lengthy mountain system that serves as a continental divide and extends from New Mexico to Alaska. Somewhat surprisingly, the Continental Divide reaches its highest elevations within Colorado, making it the "most elevated" state with an approximate mean altitude of 6,800'.[1] On or near the Divide are most of Colorado's "fourteeners," 53 peaks whose summits exceed 14,000'. Prior to Alaskan statehood in 1959, Colorado claimed more than three-fourths of the

nation's fourteeners, three-fourths of all area above 10,000', and the second and third highest mountains.

More significant than altitude as an indication of the grandeur of the Colorado Rockies, however, is relief — the differences in elevation between peaks and nearby lowlands. The contrasts are especially striking along the east face of the Front Range where the 12,500-foot Continental Divide is only 20 miles west of the Boulder Valley (5,000'), or where Longs Peak (14,256') towers 9,000' above the adjacent plains. Equally impressive are the fourteeners of the Sawatch Range viewed from the Arkansas Valley or the jagged crest of the Sangre de Christos framing the San Luis Valley on the east.

Impressively sculpted by water, ice, and wind, the mountains encompass the great diversity of landforms created by the interplay of these surface agents with underlying bedrock. Geologically new, the Southern Rockies are products of widespread crustal upheaval that affected western North America about 60 million years ago. Horizontal sedimentary rocks were arched and later eroded to reveal a hard rock core of igneous and metamorphic rocks. Repeated cycles of uplift and erosion created and destroyed ancestral mountains where today's ranges exist. Structurally, with the exception of the San Juan Mountains, these ranges are roughly anticlinal with crystalline cores and flanked by dipping sedimentary rocks.[2]

Geographically, they are not a single barrier, but rather consist of two series of ranges that are roughly parallel (*en echelon*) and separated by downwarped and faulted basins known as parks: North Park, Middle Park, South Park, and the San Luis Valley. These expansive, treeless, intermontane lowlands so impressed explorer John Wesley Powell that he identified the Southern Rockies as the Park Mountains on his regional map of the United States.[3]

Weathering and erosion of the anticlinal mountains gave rise to three distinct geomorphic zones: the foothills, the lower mountains, and the "high country." Many ranges are flanked by a narrow fringe of parallel ridges called hogbacks. Resistant sandstones

characteristically cap these linear features, typically asymmetrical in profile with the steeper slope facing the mountains and occasionally intricately eroded into sandstone wedges or "flatirons."

The lower mountains or montane zone stretches from about 6,000' to 10,500'. It has undergone varying degrees of dissection by streams originating in the high country and is characterized by deep, narrow canyons, steep slopes, and, in many areas, by fairly wide, gently undulating divides. In many respects, these coniferous cloaked highlands are reminiscent of the White Mountains of New Hampshire or the Adirondacks of New York.

The high country is distinct: bold, rocky, rugged, and dotted with lakes. Alpine (valley) glaciers have transformed an otherwise uninspiring landscape into a spectacular array of steep headwalls, comb ridges, lake basins, fjord-like valleys, and morainal ridges. A few small glaciers still survive in protected north and east facing cirques, rem-

[1]Franklin K. Van Zandt, "Boundaries of the United States and the Several States," Geological Survey Professional Paper 909, Government Printing Office (1976), p. 176.

[2]William D. Thornbury, *Regional Geomorphology of the United States* (New York: John Wiley and Sons, 1965), p. 334.

[3]John Wesley Powell, "Physiographic Regions of the United States," National Geographic Society Monograph 3 (1895), pp. 65–100.

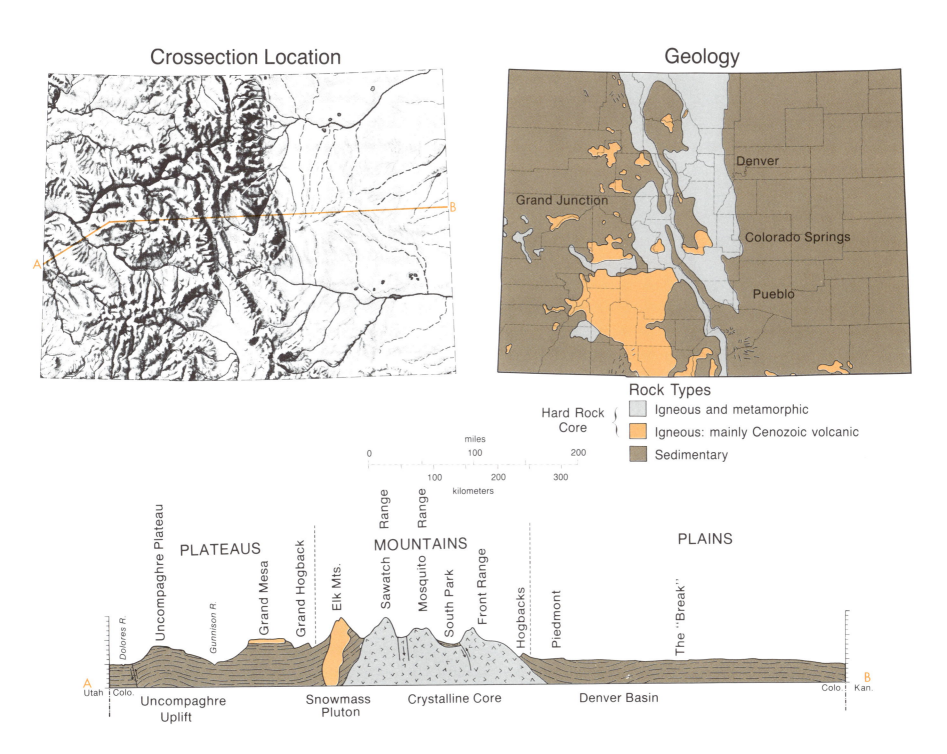

Crossection Location

Geology

Grand Junction

Denver

Colorado Springs

Pueblo

Hard Rock Core

Rock Types

Igneous and metamorphic

Igneous: mainly Cenozoic volcanic

Sedimentary

miles
0   100   200

100   200   300
kilometers

PLATEAUS

Uncompaghre Plateau

Dolores R.

Gunnison R.

Grand Mesa

Grand Hogback

Elk Mts.

Sawatch Range

Mosquito Range

South Park

Front Range

MOUNTAINS

Hogbacks

Piedmont

PLAINS

The "Break"

A
Utah | Colo.

Uncompaghre Uplift

Snowmass Pluton

Crystalline Core

Denver Basin

B
Colo. | Kan.

Crossection A-B

Crossection scale
1 in. = 50 miles
1 cm = 32 km

COLORADO GEOLOGY

5

nants of ice tongues that once were hundreds of feet thick and 10–15 miles in length. Most of Colorado's natural lakes occupy small ice-scoured basins at the heads of glaciated valleys or impounded depressions (e.g., Twin Lakes and Grand Lake) behind morainal debris at lower elevations.

It is erroneous to assume that all of the high country was glaciated. Extensive areas of the highest divides, now gently rolling tundra, were untouched. These broad, flat-topped surfaces are a puzzlement to both natives and tourists who are astonished to find some of the most easily traversed country at the highest altitudes.

The Plateaus. Approximately one-fourth of Colorado, from the base of the Rockies westward to the Utah border, has landscapes that are geomorphically repetitive. The region should not be visualized as a single plateau but as an irregular step-like surface composed of mesas and plateaus of varying sizes and altitudes. Colorado National Monument outside of Grand Junction is a microcosm of this geomorphology. Within its limited confines, many representative landforms and rock types are strikingly visible. A partial list includes:

1. Timber covered mesas rimmed with resistant caprock;
2. Deeply incised canyons;
3. Individual rock spires (monoliths);
4. Layer-cake-like exposures of multicolored sedimentary rock resting on an ancient (pre-Cambrian) crystalline complex;
5. Intricate erosion and weathering of beds of varying resistances into beehives, arches, windows, turtlebacks, and balanced rocks;
6. Tilted sedimentaries converted into flat-irons; and
7. A striking escarpment rising sharply from the Colorado River Valley.

Plateau profile

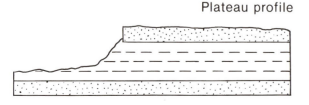

The distinctive angular forms of mesas and plateaus are encountered repetitively in the drylands of the West. In cross section three characteristic slopes are revealed:

1. A broad, flattish summit;
2. A precipitous face or rimrock normally sandstone but possibly limestone or basalt; and
3. A moderately steep basal slope underlain by weak shale.

This typical profile forms one or more edges of such well known features as Grand Mesa, Battlement Mesa, Mesa Verde, Yampa Plateau, Roan Cliffs, Book Cliffs, and Paradox Valley.

The Colorado River and its tributaries have differentially eroded the plateaus. In some locales, wide floodplains and open lowlands such as the Grand and Uncompahgre valleys provide fertile soils for agriculture and corridors for rails and roads. Elsewhere a combination of local uplift and subsequent downcutting by streams has created a maze of entrenched canyons that seriously impede transportation.

The basic horizontality of mesas and plateaus should not lead to the assumption that all of western Colorado is underlain by horizontal rock. As suggested above, a gentle warping of sedimentary rock over large distances has produced substantial changes in the altitude of some beds. For instance, the Kaibab limestone is 5,000' above sea level in the Uncompahgre Upwarp, 9,000' below sea level in the Piceance Basin, and 5,000' below sea level in the San Juan Basin. These structural basins have significant accumulations of mineral fuels, notably petroleum, oil shale, and coal.

The Plains. Stretching eastward and gradually downward for approximately 150 miles from the mountain front, the lowlands of Colorado are higher than many hilly or mountainous regions elsewhere in the United States. Appropriately, geomorphologists have labeled this surface the High Plains. Typically, elevations average about 4,200' in eastern Colorado and 5,000'–6,000' along the plains/mountains contact. Elevations are

Mountains

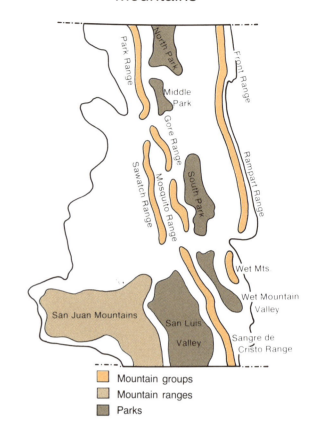

- ■ Mountain groups
- ■ Mountain ranges
- ■ Parks

Plateau Country

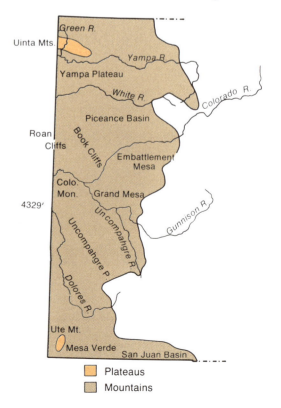

- ■ Plateaus
- ■ Mountains

Plains

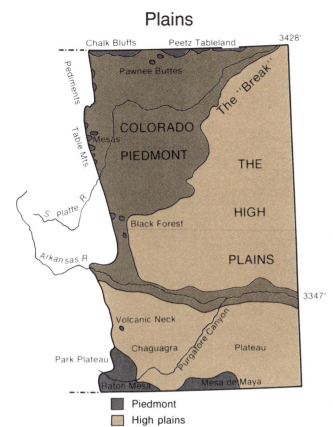

Piedmont
High plains
Rugged periphery

lowest where the South Platte and Arkansas Rivers cross the state line (about 3,400') and highest in the Black Forest where the divide between the two drainages exceeds 7,500'.

Structurally, simplicity characterizes this region. Sedimentary rocks generally prevail as a thick veneer (10,000'–12,000') which is essentially horizontal in the east and gently downwarped near the mountains. The large structural depressions (geosynclines) have yielded significant quantities of coal, petroleum, and natural gas while the horizontal porous sandstones (notably, the Ogallala formation) are major aquifers.

The surfaces of the High Plains may appear monotonous and uninspiring to the non-discerning. Careful examination, however, reveals significant regional contrasts. At the base of the mountains, the Platte and Arkansas rivers have removed a substantial portion of the younger rock creating an erosional lowland—the Colorado Piedmont. To the east, a very subtle break, a 20–25' escarpment, separates the piedmont from the relatively undissected, unbroken plains. Local relief is minimal, with portions of this surface "flatter than a pancake." Only the curvature of the Earth limits the range of visibility, unless conspicuous features such as Pikes Peak, which is visible from Firstview 135 miles to the east, tower above the horizon.

Contrasting markedly and fringing the piedmont and High Plains are a variety of landforms of considerable relief. In the north at Pawnee Buttes, two resistant sandstone remnants are vivid evidence of formerly more extensive Cretaceous rocks. Along the Front Range gravel-capped mesas (pediments) and occasional volcanic flows, dikes, and necks rise abruptly above the valley floors as at Rocky Flats northwest of Denver, Valmont Butte (dike) east of Boulder, and Table Mountain astride Clear Creek in Golden. In the south volcanic highlands extend from Trinidad to the Oklahoma line, sharply separating the plains of Colorado from New Mexico. These highly eroded and canyoned flattops have local relief differences of up to 4,000'.

With the exception of its rugged perimeter, the High Plains is home for most Coloradans. Either they are widely dispersed as farmers, ranchers, or dwellers in small supply centers or they are densely concentrated in the river valleys of the piedmont. This gently undulating, well-watered lowland has become Colorado's heartland containing 83% of its people, 90% of its manufacturing, and most of its irrigation agriculture. To a lesser degree, western valleys—the Colorado, Yampa, White, Uncompahgre, and Gunnison —have similar population nodes. These concentrations within the plateaus and on the plains exist mainly because of their propitious locations, where water that accumulates on and flows from the mountain roof may be diverted for agricultural, industrial, and domestic use.

Mountain Glaciation

THE POPULAR IMAGE OF a mountain landscape relies on the striking relief that nature's erosive processes create, a beautiful irony born of environmental degradation. Nowhere is the irony more evident than in Colorado's Rocky Mountains, where the destructive power of running water has been enhanced by moving ice. In this sense, the Rockies share alpine features with other famous middle and high latitude highlands, such as the Sierra Nevada, Cascades, the Himalayas, Norway, and Switzerland. In each case, glaciers shaped intricate networks of sharp peaks, sawtooth ridges, bowl-like basins, and steepwalled valleys.

Simply put, glaciation is possible when winter snows persist through the summer into the following winter. A cooler summer or perhaps a wetter winter allows a few inches of snow to carry over. In mountainous terrain the zone of initial ice accumulation, the *névé*, forms somewhere below the summit, likely on the poleward slope, where the combination of precipitation and coolness creates a favorable environment for snow retention. A thousand years of slightly cooler or wetter conditions translate into a deep ice mass, the bottom layers of which represent snow that fell 1,000 years before. Lengthen the time and the mass is large enough to cool the microclimate, reflect solar radiation, and promote further growth. The snow is then deep enough to compress the lower layers until they behave like a super-cooled plastic and begin movement outward and downward. Finally, long-term variations in climatic conditions produce numerous advances and retreats of the glacial lobes.

During the Ice Age, the Pleistocene Epoch, cordilleran ice sheets developed over high mountain zones while great continental ice sheets spread southward over northern Europe and North America. Tongues of ice followed existing stream-cut valleys downslope to about 8,000' in the Colorado Rockies. In the Front Range, glaciers at maximum development reached present-day Nederland,

Estes Park, and Grand Lake. The map at lower left outlines the maximum extent of ice and the lowlands affected by outwash during the one million years of the Pleistocene. Approximately 7,000 years ago, at the outset of the warm "altithermal" in the Southwest, glaciers probably disappeared in the Front Range and retreated markedly in Colorado's other high mountain areas. Except for some minor glacial advances (the Neoglaciation) in historic times, modern warmth severely limits the actual area of ice, mere remnants of once-extensive alpine glaciers that etched the high country.

At the source, the névé, the glaciers begin their destruction of the water-cut uplands. Summer meltwater refrozen to contact rock surfaces fractures the rock along joints, and moving slightly, pulls or plucks rock fragments from the contact surface. Given enough time the ice masses begin the relentless excavation of bedrock, causing ever-greater amphitheaters to grow back toward the summits. Surrounding sheets tighten the ring of excavation. The great cusps that result, called *cirques*, produce serrated rock ridges (*arêtes*) as they merge with one another. Remnant summits, plucked from all sides, take on spire-like shapes called *horns*.

As the ice moves over the cirque threshold and downslope, the gouging, grinding, cutting, polishing, and bulldozing continues. Giant boulders, frozen into slowly moving ice, grind and twist to produce great faceted chunks of rock deposited far from their source. Ice-locked rock and clay plane and polish the bedrock they override. Ice tongues pushing outward and downward cut V-shaped valleys into U-shaped glacial troughs and leave remnant spurs between the troughs. The moving glacial mass, like a huge conveyor belt, internally moves debris toward its terminus and edges creating mounds and ridges of unsorted rocks, gravels, and clay called *moraines*. Downstream beyond the glacier, streams swollen by meltwater carry boulders and rock "flour" far out onto the lowlands where outwash plains are built.

Retreating glaciers, pausing occasionally, deposit recessional moraines over the previously scoured bedrock. In the aftermath, the

older stream system, now deranged by glacial activity, becomes marked by waterfalls and rapids. Lakes fill depressions behind moraines or in bedrock pockets scoured out by moving ice. Small round, clear, rock-bottom lakes (*tarns*) typically occupy the cirque basins, surrounded on three sides by steep headwalls.

Reclothed in forest and tundra and mantled with winter snow, the final product is a rugged, rocky landscape captured in our image of the mountains.

Pleistocene Glaciation

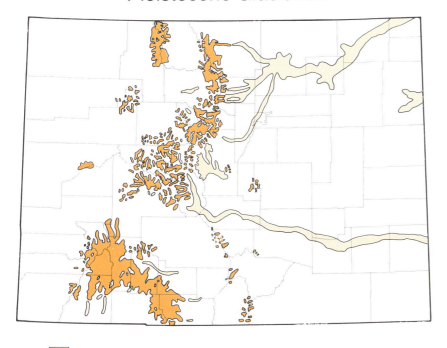

Lands occupied by glaciers

Glacial outwash and sediments

Mountain Glaciation

Source: Geological Society of America "Glacial Map of North America" (1945)

Vegetation

ITHIN COLORADO'S 104,247 square miles can be found four of the planet's major vegetation types: grasslands, desert shrub and brushlands, coniferous forests, and alpine tundra.

Grasslands. The Colorado portion of the great North American grassland is commonly referred to as shortgrass prairie or steppe, clearly distinguishing it from the tall grass prairie of the more humid continental interior. To the layman, the High Plains and mountain parks are simply vast expanses of grass, but botanists make significant regional distinctions by identifying and mapping dominant species. The layman's "sea of grass" is a complex ecosystem with conspicuously distinct sub-regions that include: 1.) most of eastern Colorado; 2.) the sandhills, especially along the Big Sandy, South Platte, and Arkansas Rivers; 3.) South Park, Wet Mountain Valley, and the periphery of the San Luis Valley; and 4.) North Park, Middle Park, and the Gunnison Basin.

Before the arrival of the white man, these open, semiarid grasslands supported an abundance of wildlife and provided a home for nomadic plains Indians. But in less than half a century (c. 1860–1910), farmers and ranchers drastically altered these landscapes by breaking the sod, diverting streams, and replacing the decimated herds of buffalo and antelope with cattle and sheep. Fortunately, a reasonable perception of the "virginal" steppe may be gleaned from either the Paw-

nee or Comanche National Grasslands, protected tracts that are gradually reverting to their natural condition.

Desert Shrublands and Brushlands. Very little of the state is classified as desert—areas where evaporation greatly exceeds limited quantities of precipitation; in Colorado rainfall on the desert border is approximately 10" annually. High aridity deters the growth of grasses in favor of drought-resistant shrubs and brush. Small portions of northwest and southwest Colorado, the lower White River, and the lower reaches of the Colorado, Gunnison, and Uncompahgre Rivers are dominated by shadscale interspersed with rabbit brush, greasewood, galletas, and other grasses. The highly alkaline soils of the San Luis Valley support thinly cloaked brushlands dominated by greasewood intermixed with rabbit brush, saltbush, wheatgrass, sedges, and rushes. Between these harsh environments and the wooded landscapes of the plateaus and mountains, desert shrubs and brush give way to sagebrush steppe with varying proportions of big sagebrush, wheatgrass, bluegrass, needle grass, Indian rice, and forbs.

Coniferous Forests. Woodland covers approximately 40% of the state—particularly the land above 5,000', except for parks and tundra. The composition and appearance (physiognomy) of this coniferous cover changes drastically with increasing elevation from open stands of piñon pine and juniper or occasional thickets of gambel oak to increasingly denser forests of ponderosa pine and Douglas-fir. At approximately 11,000'

climatic severity limits the growth of upright timber, gradually decreasing its height and girth and eventually limiting survival to discontinuous clumps or windrows of gnarled and stunted growth called *krummholz*.

Tundra. Above 11,500' the gnarled and stunted krummholz gives way to alpine tundra, a life zone distinguished by the absence of upright timber or tall shrubs. From a distance, it appears as a rather homogeneous expanse of low plants. Closer inspection reveals a striking heterogeneity of plant life influenced by snow cover, exposure, wind, drainage, soil characteristics, animal burrows, and other environmental controls. Their overall impact creates a complex mosaic of vegetation units (*stand types*) that vary in area from a few square inches to more than one acre. Generally, tundra is dominated by low, perennial sedges, grasses, herbs, and minute shrubs that many refer to as "alpine grassland." Wildlife is not abundant in this zone of extreme cold, high winds, a brief growing season, and permanently frozen subsoil (*permafrost*). However, it is the habitat for all or part of the year for bighorn sheep (state mammal), marmot, pocket gopher, pika, and ptarmigan.

SELECTED REFERENCES

Daubenmire, R. F. "Vegetational Zonation in the Rocky Mountains," *The Botanical Review,* Vol. IX, No. 6 (1943): 325–393.

Natural Vegetation, Colorado, Map M7-E-22390, Soil Conservation Service, U.S. Department of Agriculture, 1972.

Weber, William A. *Rocky Mountain Flora* (Boulder: Colorado Associated University Press, 1976).

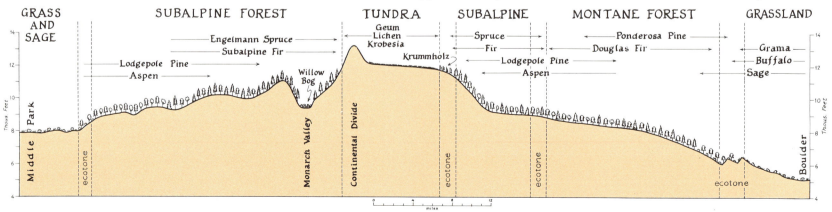

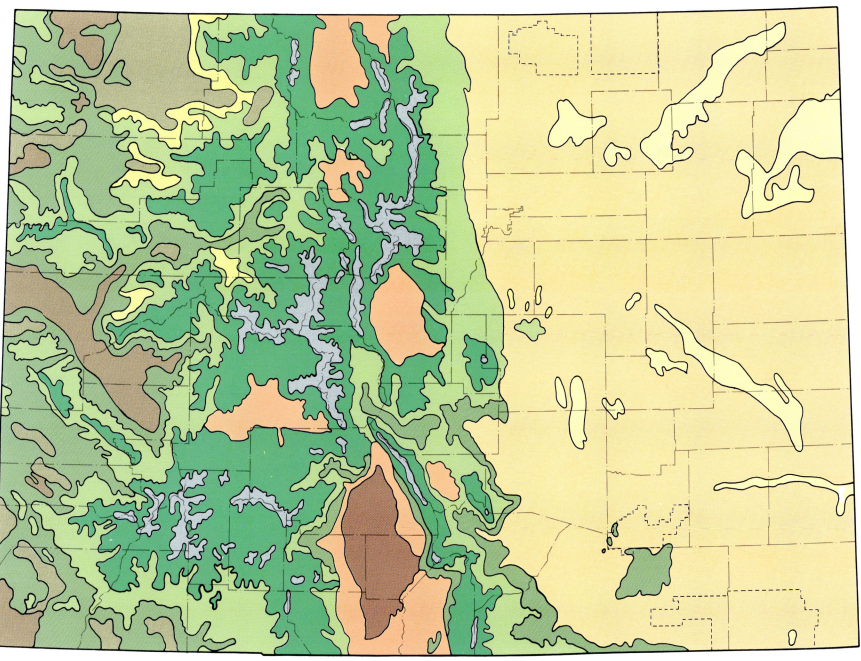

Vegetation Types

Grasslands: plains	Oakbrush: plateau and foothills
Grasslands: sand hills	Woodlands: lower mountains
Grassland and sagebrush: mtn. parks and valleys	Woodlands: plateau and southern mountains
Shrubland: desert	Forests: high mountains
Brushland: desert	Meadows and grasslands: alpine
Sagebrush: plateau	National grasslands

NATURAL VEGETATION

miles

0		75		150
0	75	150	225	

kilometers

Soils

ONLY SINCE 1870 have soils been understood as individual natural bodies, each with a singular morphology stamped by the combination of climate, living matter, age, and earthy parent materials.[1] Soil development (*pedogenesis*) ideally leads to the creation of soils with well-defined layers (*horizons*) and other traits such as color, texture, hydrogen-ion level, colloidal structure, and mineral and organic content. Careful and continuing research of these properties has enabled soil scientists (*pedologists*) to establish the Comprehensive Soil Classification System (CSCS). The system's complexity and the physical diversity of Colorado create a bewildering mosaic of soil types that need generalization. For clarity and understanding, six categories have been selected for discussion.[2]

In Colorado's mountains, two soils predominate: *Cryoboralfs* in cool, humid, environments and *Pergelic Cryaguepts* in cold regions underlain with permanently frozen ground (*permafrost*). Known as Gray Wooded soils in earlier classifications, Cryoboralfs develop beneath pine, fir, and spruce forests between 6,000 and 11,000' where precipitation averages 18" to 45" annually and the mean annual temperature is in the 33° to 45°F range. These soils, which cover steep slopes and ridges, flat-topped divides, glacial moraines, and outwash, are typically characterized by moderate surface accumulation of partially decayed litter (*humus*) and by a gray, leached horizon that overlies a thin-to-thick brown lower horizon with variable degrees of soluble salts and clays. Except for providing limited grazing for livestock who browse on the new growth that follows the retreating snow line, they are not significant agriculturally because of steep slopes and a short growing season. These soils are especially important, however, for water retention (controlling runoff from melting snows and thunderstorms) and as the slightly acidic medium that supports most of Colorado's coniferous forest.

On the cold, wet, high divides and cirques above timberline, Pergelic Cryaguepts (formerly classified as tundra or alpine) soils prevail. Developing in regions of heavy snowfall, a short growing season, and under a grass-shrub cover, Pergelic Cryaguepts are typically thick-turfed and black at the surface, gray colored at depth, moderately to strongly acidic, and mineralogically similar to their parent material. These soils have appreciable microrelief because their saturation from thaw and snowmelt creates ideal conditions for frost heave, solifluction, and soil creep—movements that produce terraces, rock rings, polygons, and stone strips. This landscape, significant for its recreational and grazing values, serves as the state's major snowshed. The distinct turf horizon provides an optimum infiltration surface, storing and gradually discharging meltwater for stream flow during the summer months.

The rugged, semiarid to subhumid plateaus of western Colorado and the well-dissected southern plains are, to a large degree, covered with poorly developed soils on actively eroding slopes. Called *Torriorthents*, they tend to be dry and calcareous with little carbonaceous material and lacking well-developed horizons. Natural vegetation consists mostly of xerophytes, shrubs, and ephemeral grasses. They are seldom cultivated and are used mainly for grazing.

More productive are the soils of eastern Colorado, now designated as *Argids* and formerly classified as brown or chestnut brown soils. They form under ephemeral grasses, forbs, and scattered cacti where the climate is cool and semiarid (40°–52°F mean annual temperature and 10"–16" annual precipitation). Limited moisture and sparse vegetation restrict leaching and create their typical light coloring (as contrasted to black soils rich in organic matter) and their neutral to slight alkalinity. If carefully cultivated and moderately blessed with moisture they produce modest yields of small grains in summer fallow farming or serve as moderate quality grazing land. If slopes are gentle and if surface or underground water is available they will produce a wide variety of crops including sugar beets, alfalfa, and corn.

Near the Kansas–Nebraska boundary and in limited areas of the plateau, *Ustolls* (chestnut soils) border upon the drier Argids. Ustolls are the dark-colored, base-rich soils of the steppes. However, like their drier neighbors they suffer from drought and wind erosion and were severely decimated during the "Dust Bowls" of the 1930s and 1950s. Like other soils in semiarid environments they are used predominantly for dryland farming and grazing, or where aquifers may be tapped for central pivot irrigation.

The arid valley floors of some parks—North Park and the San Luis Valley, for example—have stretches of saline or sodic soils known as *Natrartgids*. They tend to be highly alkaline and support salt-tolerant grasses and shrubs. This open cover provides only minimal forage for occasional rough grazing.

Taken as a whole, Colorado is not a soil-rich state because much of it is too steep, too rocky, too arid, or too windy. Nevertheless, it is an exporter of agricultural commodities and of water via its major river systems. Our agricultural, hydrological, and recreational welfare rests on careful husbandry and stewardship of the few areas that have a maturely developed "life layer."

[1]Soil Survey Staff, *Soil Taxonomy*, Agricultural Handbook No. 436. U.S. Department of Agriculture, 1975, p. 1.

[2]For detailed characteristics of the CSCS and its orders, suborders, great groups, subgroups, families, and series, refer to *Soil Taxonomy*, footnoted above.

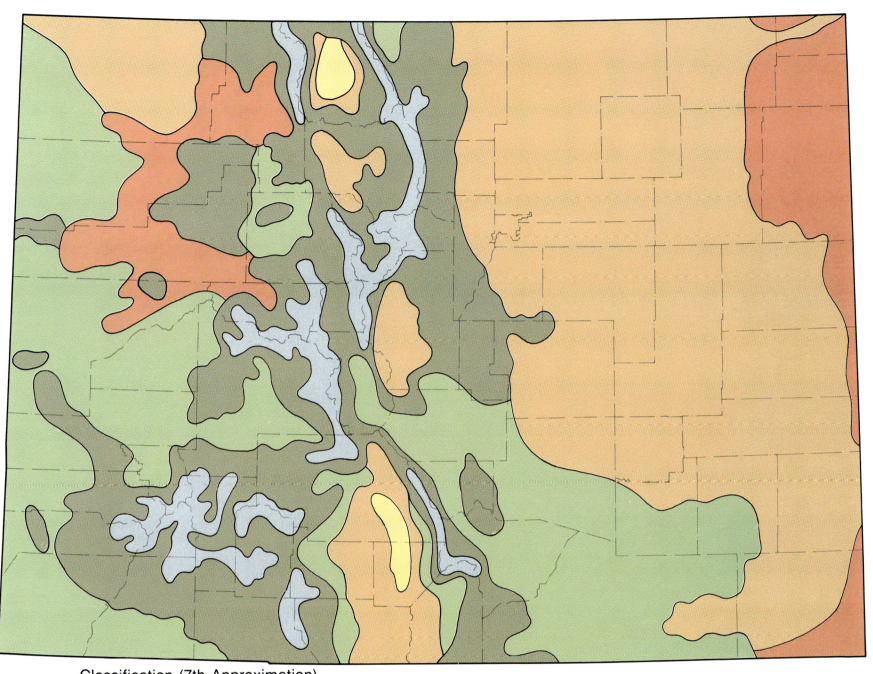

Classification (7th Approximation)

CRYOBORALFS: Gray woodland

PERGELIC CRYAQUEPTS: Tundra

TORRIORTHENTS: Lithosols, regosols

ARGIDS: Brown and chestnut brown

USTOLLS: Chestnut

NATRARGIDS: Solonetz

SOILS

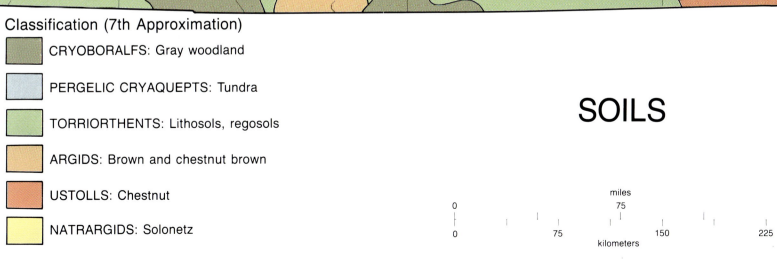

miles

0   75   150

0   75   150   225

kilometers

Climate

Although Colorado's climate varies tremendously from location to location, most Coloradans live in the semiarid lowlands, clustered in urban or agricultural oases along the South Platte, Arkansas, and Colorado river systems where annual precipitation averages 15″ or less. From mining days to the present, lowlanders have extolled Colorado's climatic virtues. These claims are somewhat justified by the climatic record, with Denver comparing favorably with other U.S. cities at approximately the same latitude (Table 1).

However, a balanced assessment reveals that Denver is not immune to sub-zero cold waves, high winds, temperature inversions, 100° summer days, or damaging torrential downpours. With the exception of temperature inversions and associated air pollution, these weather hazards are relatively uncommon events that do not detract appreciably from the overall quality and desirability of the plains climate.

Mountain climates are more complex owing to the interplay of two principles of mountain geography. The first, the principle of vertical differentiation, explains how altitude markedly influences temperature, precipitation, pressure, and other climatic elements. Temperature decreases with increasing elevation at an average rate of 3.3°F per 1,000′ or 1°C per 100 meters. Not unexpectedly, Leadville at 10,000′ has a January temperature average of 17°F as compared to 33°F in Denver at 5,300′. Precipitation increases with increasing elevation. Air crossing the Rockies and high plateaus rises, expands, and cools, usually inducing condensation in the form of clouds or fog and frequently yielding precipitation in the form of snow or rain. Pressure decreases with altitude at approximately 1/30 of its value for ever 900′ in height. Mile-high Denver has an average of 25.3″ of mercury compared to a sea level average of 29.92″. At higher altitudes, such as 10,000′ with pressure of about 20″, many individuals suffer "mountain sickness" or a general debilitation from the lack of oxygen.

The zonation of temperature, precipitation, and other elements is clearly indicated by the closely spaced isolines which outline the major mountain ranges as cool, wet, verdant islands set in a sea of semiaridity. Careful analysis of the data reveals three climatic zones — *Montane, Subalpine,* and *Alpine* — whose altitudinal limits and characteristics will vary considerably because of differences in latitude, exposure to prevailing winds, and air mass dominance (Table 2).

The second principle of mountain geography, "spotty distribution," converts each zone into a complicated mosaic dominated by common climatic traits, but pocked with miniature enclaves with locally distinct climates. The subhumid to humid montane zone, for example, characteristically supports ponderosa pine forest. However, on shaded, north-facing slopes where evapotranspiration rates are less, dense stands of Douglas-fir and spruce flourish. South-facing slopes, exposed to intense solar radiation, are substantially drier in terms of available moisture and support scattered pines in a predominantly grassy environment.

The distinctive north/south lineation of mountain climates grades into highly irregular patterns in western plateaus or into roughly elliptical patterns in the high parks. Vertical differentiation prevails but is strikingly modified by an intricately and dendritically[1] dissected landscape of canyons, mesas, plateaus, and basins and by distance and isolation from sources of moisture.

At lower elevations or in enclosed basins, arid, semiarid, or subhumid conditions prevail. Aridity occurs in the mountain-rimmed San Luis Valley, along the lower Colorado and Uncompahgre rivers, and in extreme southwest Colorado where annual precipitation averages less than 10″. Semiaridity is associated with North, Middle, and South parks, much of northwest Colorado, and a lowland fringe south and west of the San Juan Mountains. Sub-humid climates with enough precipitation (15–20″) to support an open woodland of juniper and piñon pine or scrub oak are widespread at intermediate elevations from New Mexico to Wyoming (e.g., Mesa Verde or the Yampa Plateau). Higher plateaus with extensive summit areas, such as the Uncompahgre and White, are sufficiently humid and cool for montane and subalpine forests.

Western Coloradans, like their eastern counterparts, are concentrated in urban and agricultural oases along major rivers in climatically desirable but moisture-deficient environments. Their winters are slightly cooler and their summers are as warm or slightly warmer than those in the Colorado Piedmont (Table 3). The Grand Valley, how-

[1]Dendritic drainage, frequently associated with horizontal sedimentary or massive igneous rock, has a tree-like or finger-like pattern in plain view.

Table 1. CLIMATIC DATA FOR SELECTED CITIES
near the 40th parallel

City	Alt. Feet	Ave. Monthly Temp. °F Cold Mon.	Warm Mon.	Annual Precip.	Rel. Humid. %	Poss. Sun %	Precip. Days
Denver	5,283	29.9	73.0	15.5″	53	70	88
Kansas City	1,014	27.8	78.8	37.0″	68	67	97
Philadelphia	5	32.3	76.8	39.9″	66	58	116
San Francisco	53	50.9	62.2	20.7″	71	67	67

Table 2. MOUNTAIN CLIMATES

	Altitudinal Ranges	Temps. Jan.	Ave. July	Precip. Ave. Annual	Vegetation
Montane	5,500– 9,000	20–30°	60–70°	18–25″	Ponderosa pine & Douglas-fir
Subalpine	9,000–11,500	10–20°	50–60°	25–35″	Spruce and balsam fir
Alpine	above 11,500	0–10°	40–50°	30–60″+	Tundra

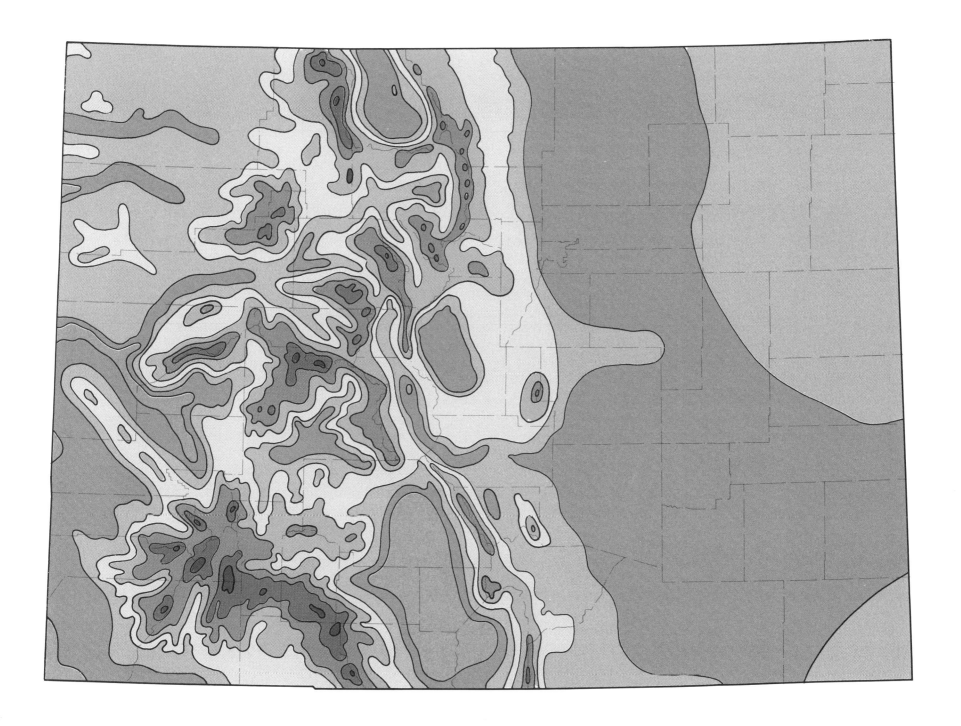

Annual Totals (inches)

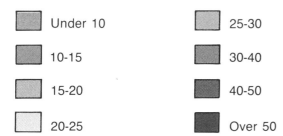

Under 10		25-30	
10-15		30-40	
15-20		40-50	
20-25		Over 50	

AVERAGE ANNUAL
PRECIPITATION

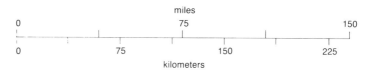

January Average Temperature (°F)

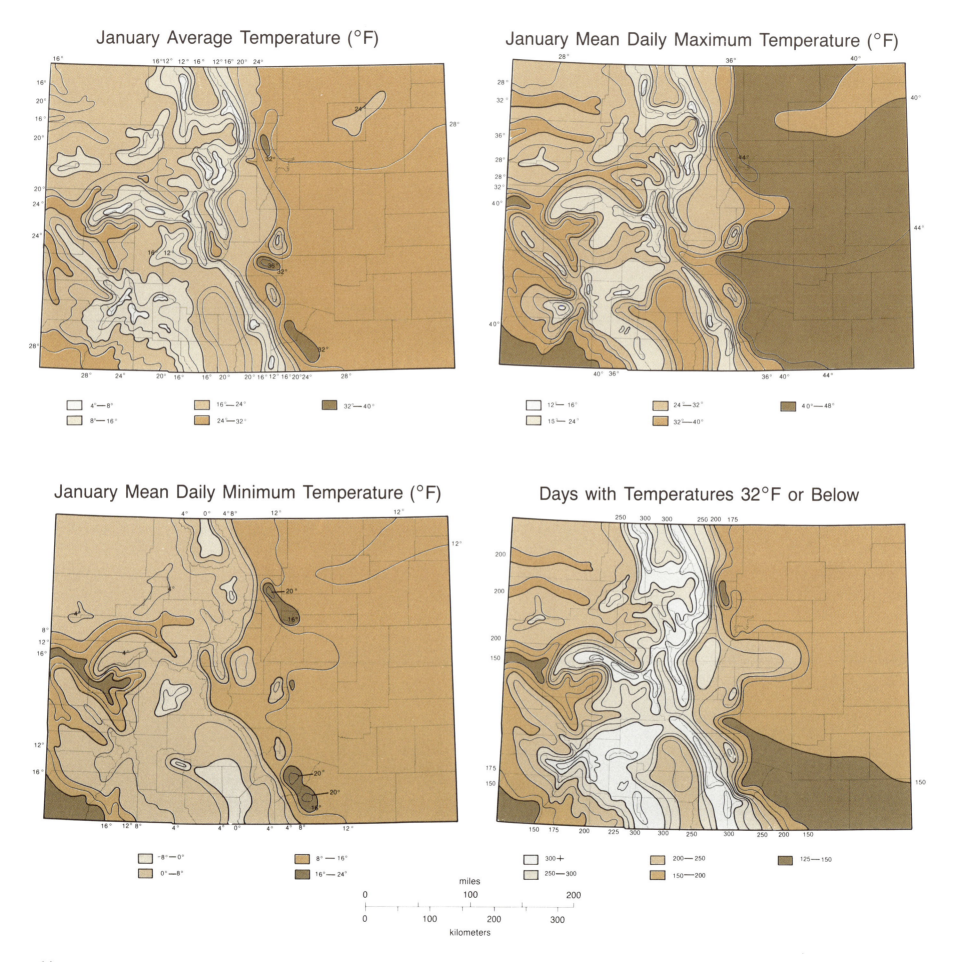

4°—8° 8°—16° 16°—24° 24°—32° 32°—40°

January Mean Daily Maximum Temperature (°F)

12°—16° 16°—24° 24°—32° 32°—40° 40°—48°

January Mean Daily Minimum Temperature (°F)

-8°—0° 0°—8° 8°—16° 16°—24°

Days with Temperatures 32°F or Below

300+ 250—300 200—250 150—200 125—150

miles
0   100   200

0   100   200   300
kilometers

July Average Temperature (°F)

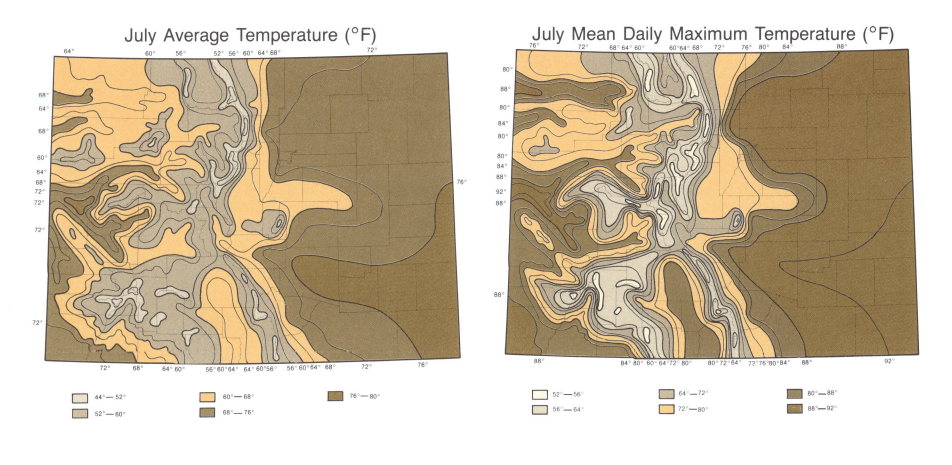

July Average Temperature (°F)

▢ 44°—52°	▢ 60°—68°	▢ 76°—80°
▢ 52°—60°	▢ 68°—76°	

July Mean Daily Maximum Temperature (°F)

▢ 52°—56°	▢ 64°—72°	▢ 80°—88°
▢ 56°—64°	▢ 72°—80°	▢ 88°—92°

July Mean Daily Minimum Temperature (°F)

Days with Temperatures 90°F or Over

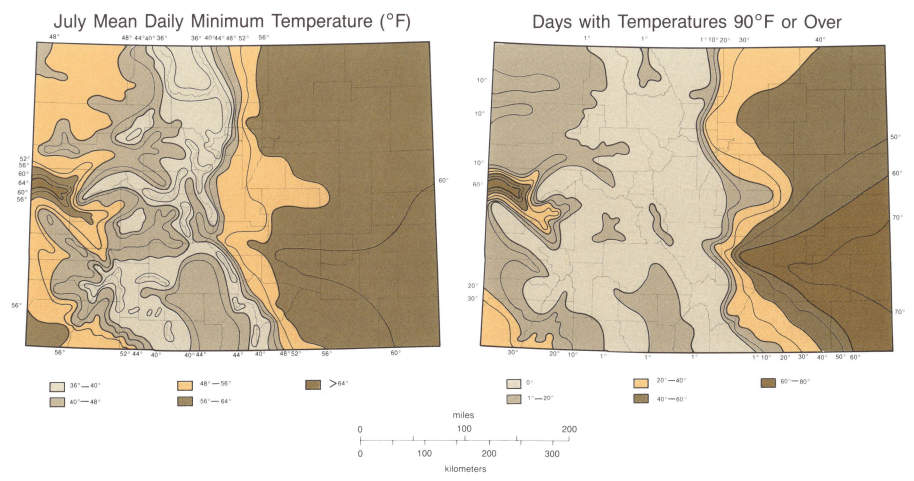

July Mean Daily Minimum Temperature (°F)

▢ 36°—40°	▢ 48°—56°	▢ >64°
▢ 40°—48°	▢ 56°—64°	

Days with Temperatures 90°F or Over

▢ 0°	▢ 20°—40°	▢ 60°—80°
▢ 1°—20°	▢ 40°—60°	

miles

0   100   200

0   100   200   300

kilometers

Table 3. EAST SLOPE-WEST SLOPE COMPARISON

City	Alt.	Temp. Jan. Ave.	July Ave.	Prcp. Ave. Annual	Grow. Season
Grand Junction	4,587'	25.0°	77.9°	8.8"	191 days
Delta	4,953'	24.6°	73.9°	8.2"	—
Paonia	5,645'	25.7°	71.0°	15.6"	—
Denver	5,283'	32.9°	74.2°	13.0"	171 days

ever, has a longer growing season and is renowned for its apple, peach, pear, and cherry orchards which are protected by the Rocky Mountain barrier from late spring or early fall incursions of cold polar air.

Both regions augment the meager amounts of precipitation by diverting water for domestic, agricultural, and industrial uses from streams originating in the cool, humid, alpine ranges and plateaus.

Snowfall. Snow is one of Colorado's most significant natural resources. With the state's high country serving as the watershed for much of the mountain west, Colorado's abundant snowfall makes irrigated agriculture possible in areas otherwise capable of dryland farming only. Mountain snows also account in part for the state's multi-billion dollar tourist industry by providing the ski conditions for which Colorado has become famous.

How much falls? Records kept by the State Climatologist[1] for a representative period, 1951–70, reveal that average annual amounts vary substantially from place to place — from as little as 8" as the norm at Karval (Lincoln County) on the High Plains to more than 350" at Wolf Creek Pass in the rugged San Juan Mountains. Precise measurements are at best difficult, since wind, exposure, measuring instruments, experience of the observer, and other factors may have a bearing on the accumulations reported. Overall, the data are sufficiently reliable so that a cartographer with a detailed knowledge of the state can convert them into a reasonably accurate snowfall map.

[1] John F. Benci and Thomas B. McKee. Colorado Monthly Temperature and Precipitation Summary for Period 1951-70. Climatology Report No. 77-1. Colorado Climatology Office, Colorado State University, Fort Collins, Colorado.

The map reveals an intricate snowfall pattern that basically reflects the state's variable relief and altitudinal diversity. The eastern plains, western valleys, and mountain-rimmed parks receive less than 50" annually, with many stations recording astonishingly low amounts, such as 9" at John Martin Dam, 14" at Palisade, and 23" at Monte Vista. The plateaus and high ranges are blanketed with substantially greater accumulations that contrast dramatically with the nearby lowlands. In southern Colorado the norm for Cumbres Pass (10,222') is 267"; less than 30 miles away at Manassa (7,500') it is only 18". Similar contrasts typically prevail between the Front Range and the High Plains, between North, South, and Middle Parks and adjacent mountains, and between the high plateaus and open valleys drained by the headwaters of the Colorado, White, and Yampa rivers.

Although physical diversity creates an intricate snowfall pattern, certain generalizations can be made. First, from the Kansas–Nebraska border westward to the Rockies snowfall amounts gradually increase from 10–25" in the lower elevations to approximately 50" along the mountain front and on the Black Forest Divide — an east–west "peninsula" of timbered high ground between the Arkansas and South Platte valleys. Second, from the base of the Rockies to the western plateaus snowfall increases rapidly with increasing elevations. Lower slopes average 50–100" per year while higher elevations receive 100–200" per year with some favored locations, especially ski basins, getting substantially more. Third, the flat-topped western plateaus are moderately endowed with 50 to 100" — sufficient moisture when coupled with warm season rain to support coniferous forests.

Snow may fall in any month in the high country; at lower elevations it usually occurs from early October to late April. In many

communities at the base of the Front Range it has snowed in every month except July. Normally, on the eastern plains and western valleys, the snow-free period is long enough for the growth and harvesting of corn, wheat, barley, potatoes, deciduous fruit, and other mid-latitude crops.

Typically, heavier snows come in the late winter or early spring (February, March, and April), falling from migratory cyclonic storms and associated fronts and upslope winds. Most of these depressions originate in the North Pacific, first striking Oregon, Washington, and British Columbia and then moving southeasterly to and across Colorado. Others originate in the central Pacific and may arrive in Colorado with copious amounts of moisture via California, Nevada, and Utah. Occasionally, these slow-moving, moisture-laden, unstable storms will dump substantial quantities of snow on all or portions of the state. One particularly severe snowfall buried Silver Lake, Colorado, under 87" in 27 hours in April, 1921. If these storms intensify while moving eastward they will add to their moisture supply by attracting maritime air from the Gulf of Mexico into their counterclockwise circular rotations. This inflow creates an upslope flow with east or northeast winds that frequently brings unexpectedly heavy snows to eastern Colorado, such as the late-season blizzard (early April, 1957) that dumped 3½' of snow on the Denver-Pueblo area.

Snowfall amounts from any given meteorological situation depend on such factors as the intensity and speed of migrating low pressure cells, the stability and moisture content of the air masses, and the paths of the storms relative to terrain barriers. Most storms yield small to moderate accumulations because 1.) Colorado is far removed from major sources of moisture (the Pacific Ocean or Gulf of Mexico); 2.) a portion of the state is usually in the "snow shadow," i.e., sheltered and protected by mountain divides from passing storms and fronts; and 3.) the state is bypassed by many cyclonic circulations whose paths roughly parallel the Canadian border from the Pacific Northwest to the Great Lakes.

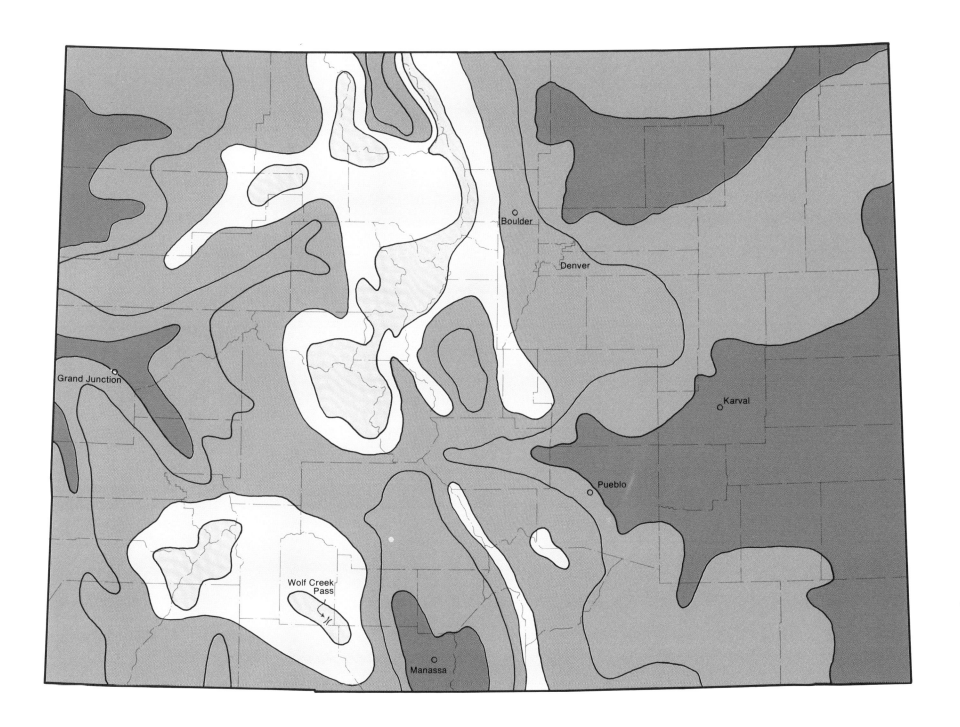

SNOWFALL
Average Annual Snowfall
1951-1970

Inches

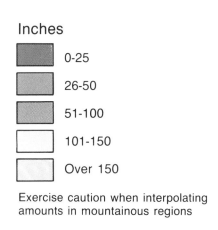

0-25

26-50

51-100

101-150

Over 150

Exercise caution when interpolating
amounts in mountainous regions

Data from Benci and McKee

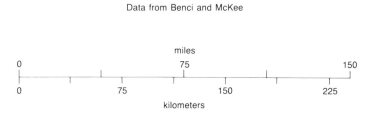

Water

Two terms—*headwaters* and *hidden waters*—highlight the nature and significance of Colorado's premier natural resource. Nourished by melting snows and modest rains along the Continental Divide and fed with additional moisture in the subalpine and montane zones, five major rivers—the North Platte, South Platte, Arkansas, Colorado, and Rio Grande—break out of their mountain ramparts onto the lower and drier plains, parks, and plateaus where they supply 3 million Coloradans with a large share of their domestic, industrial, and agricultural water. Substantial quantities, about 10 million acre-feet[1] per year, flow beyond the borders of the "headwaters state" and are tapped by urban and rural users in the grasslands and deserts of at least nine downstream states including Wyoming, Nebraska, Kansas, Oklahoma, Texas, New Mexico, Utah, Arizona, and California.

The surface flow of these streams can be readily seen and used, but less apparent (except possibly where springs emerge) are vast, hidden reservoirs of groundwater. Al-though out of sight, they have been increasingly sought as surface waters gradually become fully appropriated. Hydrologic investigations, especially in recent decades, by a wide variety of agencies and individuals have provided fairly complete data of the extent, quantity, and quality of this subterranean treasure.

The map portraying the average discharge of Colorado's rivers strikingly reveals the quantity and distribution of surface water. It also suggests the maldistribution of water and people. Relatively large amounts drain westward from the Continental Divide into the sparsely populated lands of the western mountains and plateaus while modest quantities flow through the parks and densely settled eastern valleys. The combined natural flow of the South Platte, North Platte, Arkansas, and Rio Grande is substantially less than that of the Gunnison River where it joins the Colorado River at Grand Junction. Many western streams, including the Little Snake, Yampa, White, Dolores, Animas, San Juan, Roaring Fork, or the Eagle carry comparable or greater volumes than any East Slope river.

Although the eastward draining streams provided adequate supplies to early miners, ranchers, and farmers, the burgeoning demands of irrigated agriculture and urban oases led to the appropriation of most surface water.[2] New sources were sought, especially from the relatively well-watered western slope. After acquiring water rights, usually by purchase and the right of eminent domain, eastern users divert water by ditch and tunnel across or under the Continental Divide. Most early ditch diversions supplied mining and agricultural interests, but more recent projects required the construction of large reservoirs, hard-rock tunnels, and long, wide canals. In 1980, approximately 400,000 acre-feet of west slope water, an amount comparable to the natural flow of the South Platte River, was diverted for domestic, industrial, agricultural, and power users along the Front Range corridor.[3]

Increasing demands on the surface water supply led to the exploitation of hidden or groundwater sources. Initially, most wells tapped the shallow, unconsolidated sands and gravels (*alluvial aquifers*) along the major streams. As exploration gear and drilling equipment improved, productive aquifers were detected, some in the deep fill of the San Luis and upper Arkansas valleys, others in the Ogallala Formation that underlies Eastern Colorado, or in sandstones of the Denver basin, or beneath the lower Arkansas Valley. By June 1982, approximately 150,000 wells

[1]An acre-foot is one of many standard measurements applied to water supplies. It represents the quantity needed to cover an acre (43,560 ft[2]) to a depth of 12", approximately 325,850 U.S. gallons.

[2]Colorado and most western states administer their water resources according to the Doctrine of Appropriation. "The basic concept of this doctrine is that ownership of the land provides no inherent right to water from resources upon, contiguous to, or underlying the land, but that rights to these sources are based on priority of beneficial use." Simply stated, water decrees were established by the principle of "first in time, first in right." The earliest decree (April 10, 1852) was awarded to the San Luis People's Ditch recognizing the right to divert 21 second feet from Culebra Creek and 2 second feet from Rito Seco Creek. Quote from Summary Appraisal of the Nation's Groundwater Resources—Upper Colorado Region, Geological Survey Professional Paper 813-C, p. C-33.

[3]In addition, seven projects solely on the eastern slope tap the tributaries of the North Platte River and divert 17,630 acre feet to the Cache La Poudre River in the South Platte Drainage Basin.

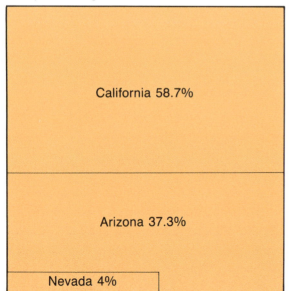

LOWER COLORADO BASIN
Annual Entitlements by State
percentage of 7.5 million acre-feet

California 58.7%

Arizona 37.3%

Nevada 4%

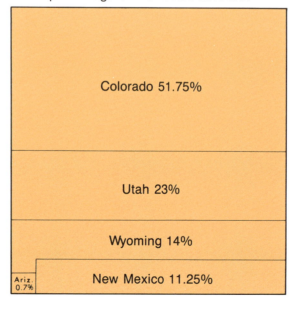

UPPER COLORADO BASIN
Annual Entitlements by State
percentage of 7.5 million acre-feet

Colorado 51.75%

Utah 23%

Wyoming 14%

Ariz. 0.7%

New Mexico 11.25%

Groundwater

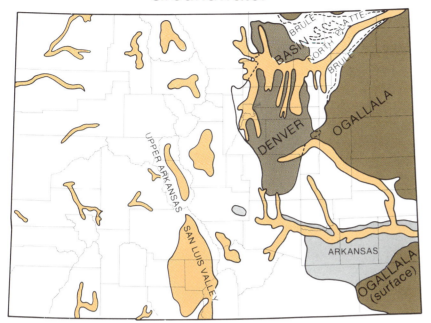

Major Sources

- ▧ Valley-fill alluvial aquifers
- ▧ Ogallala Aquifer
- ▧ Sandstone aquifers esp. Dakota Formation
- ▧ Denver Basin aquifers

Thermal Springs

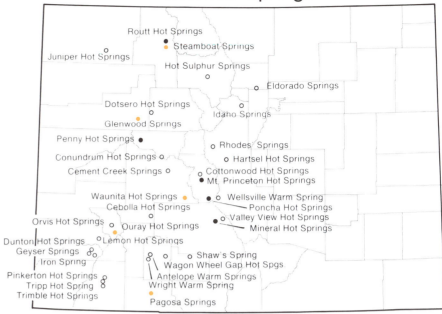

Routt Hot Springs
Steamboat Springs
Juniper Hot Springs
Hot Sulphur Springs
Eldorado Springs
Dotsero Hot Springs
Idaho Springs
Glenwood Springs
Penny Hot Springs
Rhodes Springs
Conundrum Hot Springs
Hartsel Hot Springs
Cement Creek Springs
Cottonwood Hot Springs
Mt. Princeton Hot Springs
Waunita Hot Springs
Wellsville Warm Spring
Cebolla Hot Springs
Poncha Hot Springs
Valley View Hot Springs
Orvis Hot Springs
Mineral Hot Springs
Ouray Hot Springs
Dunton Hot Springs
Lemon Hot Springs
Geyser Springs
Shaw's Spring
Iron Spring
Wagon Wheel Gap Hot Spgs
Antelope Warm Springs
Pinkerton Hot Springs
Wright Warm Spring
Tripp Hot Spring
Trimble Hot Springs
Pagosa Springs

- ● Major: high vol., high temp.
- ● Secondary: moderate vol., high temp.
- ○ Minor: small vol., variable temp.

Surface Flow

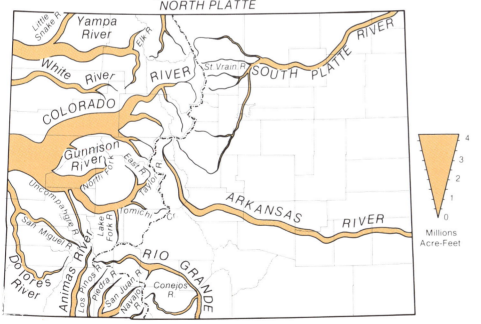

NORTH PLATTE
Little Snake R.
Yampa River
Elk R.
White River
St. Vrain R.
SOUTH PLATTE RIVER
COLORADO RIVER
Gunnison River
North Fork
East R.
Taylor R.
Lake Fork R.
Tomichi Cr.
Uncompahgre R.
San Miguel R.
ARKANSAS RIVER
Dolores River
Animas River
Los Pinos R.
Piedra R.
San Juan R.
Navajo R.
Conejos R.
RIO GRANDE

Millions Acre-Feet

WATER RESOURCES

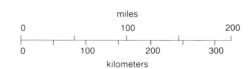

miles
0   100   200

0   100   200   300
kilometers

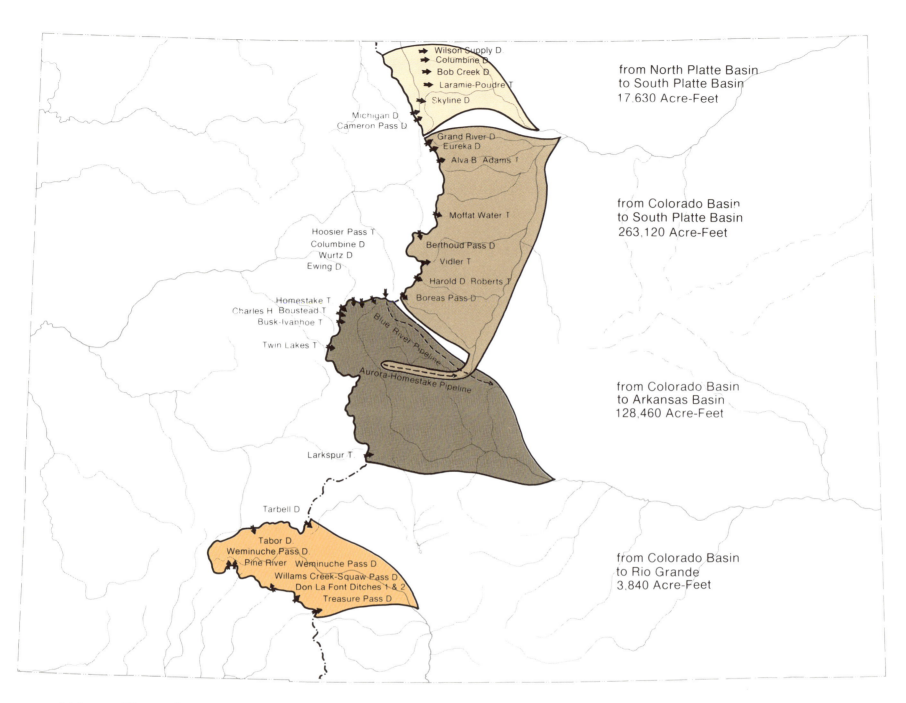

Wilson Supply D
Columbine D
Bob Creek D
Laramie-Poudre T
Skyline D

from North Platte Basin
to South Platte Basin
17,630 Acre-Feet

Michigan D
Cameron Pass D

Grand River D
Eureka D
Alva B. Adams T

from Colorado Basin
to South Platte Basin
263,120 Acre-Feet

Moffat Water T

Hoosier Pass T
Columbine D
Wurtz D
Ewing D

Berthoud Pass D
Vidler T
Harold D. Roberts T
Boreas Pass D

Homestake T
Charles H. Boustead T
Busk-Ivanhoe T

Blue River Pipeline

Twin Lakes T

Aurora-Homestake Pipeline

from Colorado Basin
to Arkansas Basin
128,460 Acre-Feet

Larkspur T

Tarbell D

Tabor D
Weminuche Pass D
Pine River   Weminuche Pass D
Willams Creek-Squaw Pass D
Don La Font Ditches 1 & 2
Treasure Pass D

from Colorado Basin
to Rio Grande
3,840 Acre-Feet

Water Transfers

From North Platte basin to
South Platte basin: 17,630 acre-feet

From Colorado basin to
South Platte basin: 263,120 acre-feet

From Colorado basin to
Arkansas basin: 128,460 acre-feet

From Colorado basin to
Rio Grande basin: 3,840 acre-feet

INTERBASIN WATER DIVERSIONS

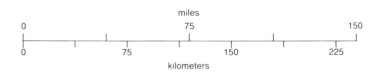

miles
0   75   150

0   75   150   225
kilometers

had been decreed, drilled, and in use.[4] Withdrawals were primarily for traditional "ditch" irrigation along the flood plains and on terraces and for new sprinkler systems, especially pivot systems that create green circles on square-mile sections of eastern Colorado.

Generally, withdrawals from deep valley fill or stream alluvium have been wisely managed and used conjunctively with surface water. Accordingly, the quantity of water in these underground aquifers has not been significantly affected. Withdrawals from the Ogallala Formation and from consolidated sandstones, however, have greatly exceeded their recharge. Water mining rather than management has severely lowered the water levels, reduced the yields, and increased extraction costs. The outlook is grim, especially for those pump irrigators in eastern Colorado who depend heavily on a rapidly dwindling resource.

Relatively insignificant in terms of flow, but very important recreationally and therapeutically are 35 thermal (hot) springs with water temperatures ranging from 79°F to 183°F. Situated mainly in the mountains, they yield approximately 11,000 gallons per minute (about 17,750 acre feet per year) of warm to hot waters that are probably heated by convecting magma. In Colorado, most springs are close to Tertiary lava flows and on or near fault zones along mountain fronts.

Two thirds of the state's geothermal discharge emanates from Glenwood Springs, Steamboat Springs, Waunita Hot Springs, Ouray Hot Springs, and Pagosa Springs, providing a variety of swimming and soaking pools, some with excellent accommodations. Five other groups of springs with smaller volumes (100–400 g.p.m.) and high temperatures are less intensively developed[5]

but have considerable economic potential. Paved roads provide easy access and the sites lie in attractive settings or command impressive mountain vistas. Historically, they have undergone varying degrees of development.

In the primary group, only Glenwood Springs has gained national recognition and acclaim. Spectacularly situated at the mouth of Glenwood Canyon and served by Interstate 70 and the mainline of the Denver and Rio Grande Railroad, this spa has become a mecca for those who ease their muscular and arthritic afflictions in the hot, mineralized baths and for thousands of tourists who relax in the warmth of an exceptionally large swimming and diving pool.

As the "headwaters state," Colorado is relatively well-endowed with surface and underground waters. Their appropriation and use, however, are not determined solely by the laws of the state. Obligations and agreements as outlined in international treaties with Mexico and compacts with downstream states must be honored. Mexico is seriously concerned and occasionally testy about the water quality and quantity as guaranteed by the treaty. Lower basin states — California, Arizona, New Mexico, and Nevada — have been apportioned, in perpetuity, exclusive beneficial use of 7.5 million acre feet annually (about ½ the normal flow) of the Colorado River system by the Colorado River Compact of 1921. The South Platte River Compact includes specific regulations concerning diversion and storage of groundwater and surface water in the lower valley. These examples suggest that the ajudication of western water resources is extremely complex. To a large degree, we can control our water destiny by wisely administering and managing those waters to which we are fully entitled.

[4]This estimate from the Office of the State Engineer, Department of Natural Resources, includes about 30,000 wells for which the paperwork is incomplete.

[5]This second group includes Mount Princeton Hot Springs, Poncha Hot Springs, Mineral Hot Springs, Routt Hot Springs, and Penny Hot Springs. A third group of 25 springs is characterized by relatively low temperatures and low volumes which limit their use for therapy and recreation.

SELECTED REFERENCES

Lewis, Robert E. "The Thermal Resources of Colorado: A Resource Appraisal." M.A. Thesis, University of Colorado, 1966.

McGuinnes, C. L. 1963. *The Role of Groundwater in the National Water Situation.* Geological Survey Water Supply Paper 1800. 1121 pp.

Pearl, Richard H. 1972. *Geothermal Resources of Colorado.* Colorado Geological Survey Special Publication 2.

Summary Appraisals of the Nation's Groundwater Resources. Geological Survey Professional Papers 813-C, 813-D, 813-H, 813-Q.

Water Resources Data for Colorado, vols. I–III, Water Year 1980, U.S. Geological Survey Water Data Report Co-80-2.

Minerals

INERAL WEALTH PROVIDED the major impetus for the settlement of Colorado. As early as 1540, Coronado searched unsuccessfully for the fabled wealth of the seven cities of Cibola. Subsequent explorers, mountain men, and prospectors failed to find the precious metals until 1858 when the Russell party struck "pay dirt" — placer gold — near the confluence of Cherry Creek and the South Platte River. In the spring of 1859, a major strike on North Clear Creek by John H. Gregory precipitated a frenzied quest for gold by thousands of miners who panned alluvial gravels for dust, flakes, or nuggets. They followed "the color" upstream and within a few years encountered the rich mother lodes of the Colorado Rockies. The search for gold led to the discovery of silver and other valuable metals including lead, zinc, and copper. By the 1890s three mining regions had evolved, each with major towns and a host of smaller settlements: 1.) the Front Range mineral belt with Central City and Leadville as the production and smelting centers for gold, silver, lead, and zinc; 2.) the San Juan region with Silverton, Telluride, and Ouray as major contributors of silver, gold, and copper; and 3.) Cripple Creek, the most productive gold district in the state.

For forty years (1880–1920), hard rock mining flourished with outputs of lead, zinc, gold, and silver reaching their highest levels

(but not simultaneously) during the four decades. Production peaks were often followed by drastic declines due to mounting costs of ore extraction, declining prices (especially for silver), and ventilation and groundwater problems in ever-deepening shafts and tunnels. Scores of once prosperous mining settlements withered or died, becoming ghost towns marked only by rusting machinery, weather-beaten buildings, or derelict and dangerous mines. Some communities continue as mining centers and county seats (Leadville and Silverton) while others with a mining past remain as county seats and now attract recreational dollars (Aspen, Breckenridge, Central City, and Telluride).

By 1920, the Colorado Rockies had yielded $1.5 billion of gold, silver, copper, lead, and zinc. The combined value of these five minerals is impressive, but more significant was the impact of their exploitation on the state: 1.) placer and lode gold attracted the "Fifty-Niners" and subsequently thousands of seekers who became the population nucleus that established Colorado as a territory in 1861 and as a state in 1876; 2.) the mining districts stimulated the growth of irrigated agriculture and ranching on the plains where many early pioneers preferred tilling the soil to working the diggings; 3.) the rules and regulations adopted in mining districts for the orderly exploitation of resources evolved into state and national mining law; 4.) the invention and subsequent manufacture in Colorado of mining machinery such as the Leyner water mining drill that permitted cleaner, faster boring and the Wilfley Table, a concentrating device for ore separation, were significant technical advances; 5.) Denver, Colorado Springs, Golden, Boulder, and other piedmont towns were established at the base of the Front Range where they functioned as supply, transportation, and smelting centers for the mining districts; 6.) the present-day accessibility of mountain valleys and slopes grows directly out of the hard rock mining, which fostered an expansive network of trails, roads, and railroads, especially narrow gauge. Modern federal, state, and county highways follow many of the older routes while others provide easy access

for hikers, anglers, and cross-country skiers into nearly every nook and cranny in the high country; 7.) the "ghosting" of Colorado has occurred on a large scale with the transformation of pristine environments into timberless, pock-marked stretches of tailings, dumps, tunnels, shafts, glory holes, and abandoned towns. The boom and bust cycles, responsible to a large degree for landscape degradations, are readily apparent (production graphs 1–5) for each precious and base metal.

Since the 1920s, fossil fuels and alloy minerals have become increasingly significant, in 1979 accounting for 83% of the total mineral value (Table 1). The sedimentary strata

Table 1. MINERAL PRODUCTION 1979
(millions of dollars)

Fuels	$1,067	
Molybdenum	604	
	$1,671	83% of total
Sand and Gravel	73	
Cement	75	
Uranium	71	
Silver	31	
	190	10% of total
Others	77	7% of total
	$1,938	100%

(soft rock) underlying the plateaus, parks, and plains yield substantial quantities of petroleum, coal, and natural gas and the crystalline core (hard rock) beneath the mountains produces 50–60% of the world's molybdenum (Graph 6). Petroleum production dates back to 1862 when A. M. Cassedy sank a discovery well on Oil Creek, six miles north of Cañon City. This success gave Colorado the distinction of being the second state in the United States to produce from drilled wells. This locale (Florence Field) accounted for most of Colorado's yield until the discoveries of the Fort Collins, Wellington, Moffat, and Iles fields in the mid-1920s. After peaking at 2,850,000 barrels in 1926, production declined until major discoveries at Rangely and Wilson Creek in the mid-40s and in the Denver basin in the early 50s led to an all-time high of 58,565,000 barrels in 1956. Yields have declined in the past two

State Total $2,159 million

Sand
Gravel
Cement

non-METALS
$165

Others

Molybdenum

METAL
$737

Others

Oil · Coal · Gas

FUELS
$1257

0   300   600   900   1200   1500

millions of dollars

Major Mining Districts

COLORADO

Central City
Georgetown
Gilman
Climax
Aspen
Leadville
Cripple Creek

MINERAL

BELT

Telluride
Ouray
Lake City
Silverton
Creede

Precious and Base Metals
Historic and Active Areas

Mineral Production 1980

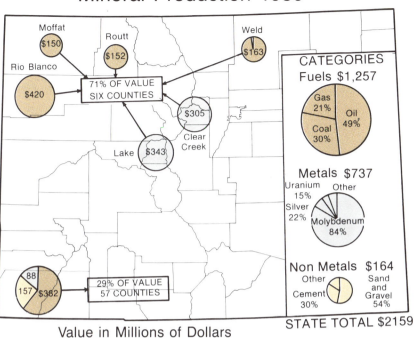

Moffat
$150

Routt
$152

Weld
$163

Rio Blanco
$420

71% OF VALUE
SIX COUNTIES

$305

Clear Creek

Lake $343

88
157 $382

29% OF VALUE
57 COUNTIES

CATEGORIES
Fuels $1,257

Gas 21%
Oil 49%
Coal 30%

Metals $737
Uranium 15%
Silver 22%
Other
Molybdenum 84%

Non Metals $164
Other
Cement 30%
Sand and Gravel 54%

STATE TOTAL $2159

Value in Millions of Dollars

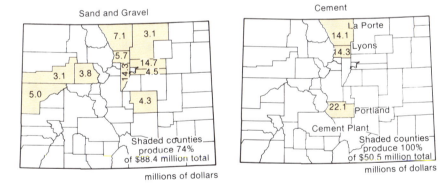

Sand and Gravel

7.1 3.1
5.7
14.3 14.7
4.5
3.1 3.8
5.0
4.3

Shaded counties
produce 74%
of $88.4 million total

millions of dollars

Cement

La Porte
14.1
Lyons
14.3

22.1 Portland
Cement Plant

Shaded counties
produce 100%
of $50 5 million total

millions of dollars

Major Non-Metallic Minerals 1980

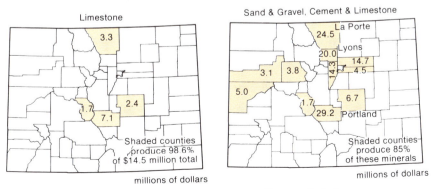

Limestone

3.3

2.4
1.7
7.1

Shaded counties
produce 98.6%
of $14.5 million total

millions of dollars

Sand & Gravel, Cement & Limestone

La Porte
24.5
Lyons
20.0
14.3 14.7
4.5
3.1 3.8
5.0
1.7 6.7
29.2 Portland

Shaded counties
produce 85%
of these minerals

millions of dollars

Numbers in counties show millions of dollars

Minerals
Production   Distribution

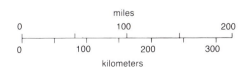

miles
0   100   200

0   100   200   300
kilometers

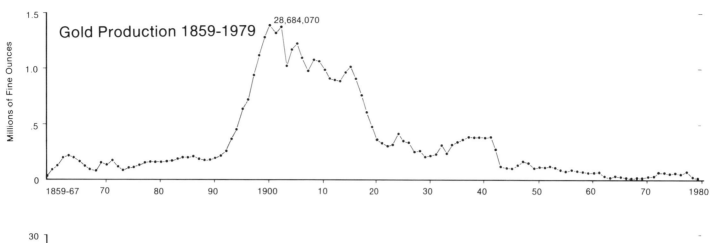

Gold Production 1859-1979

Millions of Fine Ounces

28,684,070

1859-67   70   80   90   1900   10   20   30   40   50   60   70   1980

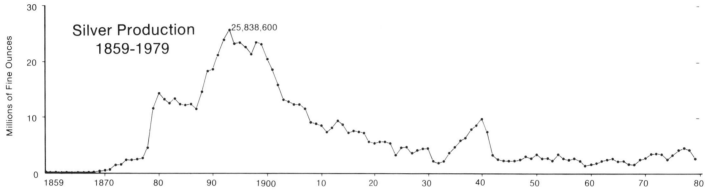

Silver Production
1859-1979

Millions of Fine Ounces

25,838,600

1859   1870   80   90   1900   10   20   30   40   50   60   70   80

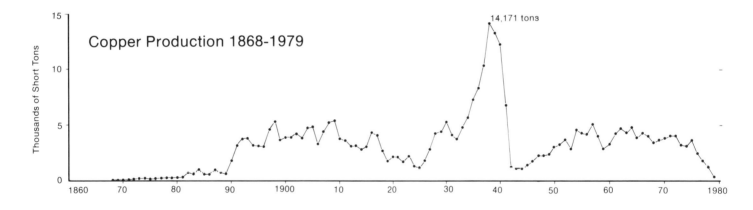

Copper Production 1868-1979

Thousands of Short Tons

14,171 tons

1860   70   80   90   1900   10   20   30   40   50   60   70   1980

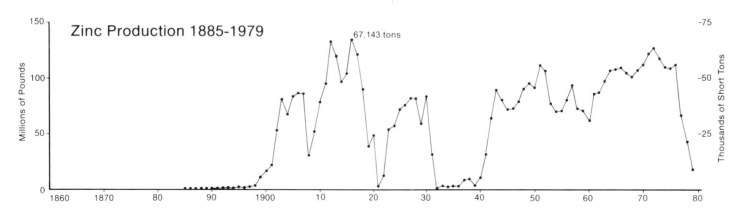

Zinc Production 1885-1979

Millions of Pounds

Thousands of Short Tons

67,143 tons

1860   1870   80   90   1900   10   20   30   40   50   60   70   80

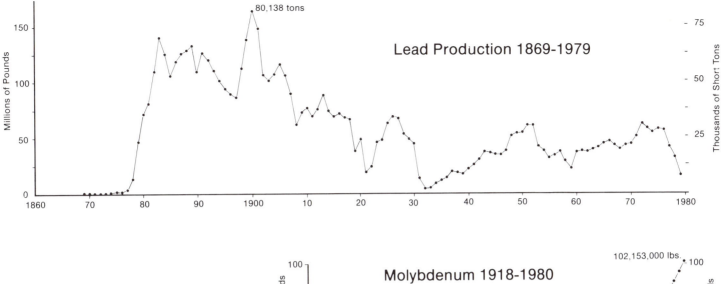

Lead Production 1869-1979

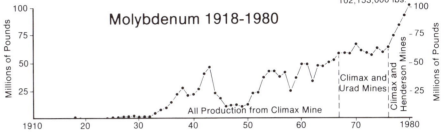

Molybdenum 1918-1980

decades to an annual production of approximately 30,000,000 barrels (Graph 7).

Coal production, unlike that of oil, has increased dramatically in recent years (Graph 8). Annual tonnages, initially peaking at over 12 million in 1917, 1918, and 1920, declined irregularly to less than 3½ million tons in the 1950s. Increasing energy demands coupled with skyrocketing prices for imported oil favored the development of extensive open pits in the 1970s, especially in Moffat and Routt Counties. Production from the new operations combined with increasing quantities from underground mines surpassed 50-year-old records in 1978 and set a new record of 18 million tons in 1979.

Natural gas, produced and used for domestic and industrial purposes since 1892 or 1893, was available in small amounts from the Boulder and Florence fields until 1923 when a discovery well by Union Oil on the Wellington Dome (Larimer County) yielded the first significant flow. Shortly thereafter, new production from the Hiawatha, Piceance Creek, and Rangely fields assured a steadily increasing supply (Graph 9), until the boom years of 1949-57. During this period, annual production jumped dramatically from 11.5

to 176.2 billion cubic feet with the completion of new wells and delivery systems in western Colorado and the Denver basin. Continued production from Adams, La Plata, Weld, Rio Blanco, and Moffat Counties, plus the recent activity in the Wattenberg Field,[1] Weld County, accounted for 81% of the state's record yield of 192 billion cubic feet in 1977.

Fossil fuels constitute 55% of the value of Colorado's mineral production, a proportion that will probably continue to increase. Coal tonnage and natural gas production are at their all-time highest levels and petroleum yields show no indication of drastic decline. The prices for these commodities continue to escalate more rapidly than those of most other minerals. In addition, the potential of oil from vast shale reserves will strengthen the position and contribution of fossil fuels to the mineral economy of the state.

Alloy minerals, molybdenum, vanadium, and tungsten, which impart hardness, toughness, and fatigue strength to steel, account for one-third of Colorado's mineral value. Molybdenum, the state's premier metal in 1979, completely dominates metallic production (83% of value) while accounting for

31% of the value of all minerals. Approximately equal tonnages are extracted from two mines, an older (1918) operation at Climax, Lake County, and a newer (1976) facility, the Henderson Mine in Clear Creek County.

Vanadium and tungsten contribute only 2.7% to the state's mineral value but they represent major domestic sources of strategic alloys, thereby reducing the steel industry's dependence on foreign ores. Production of each mineral is associated with other metals: vanadium with uranium ores[2] of the Uravan Mineral Belt of western Colorado, and tungsten as a secondary metal extracted during the processing of molybdenum ore at the Climax mine.

Uranium, considered as a metal by the Colorado Division of Mines and as a fuel since 1956 by the U.S. Bureau of Mines, would rank either as a weak second to molybdenum or a very poor fourth to coal,

[1]The Wattenberg Field accounted for 25% of the state's total in 1975.

[2]For security reasons, the U.S. Bureau of Mines and the Nuclear Regulatory Commission do not reveal the tonnage of vanadium that is extracted from carnotite, a major source of uranium.

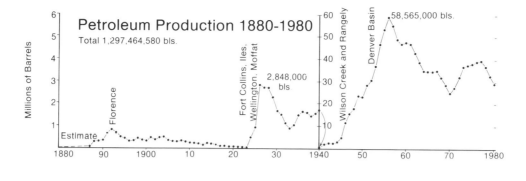

Petroleum Production 1880-1980
Total 1,297,464,580 bls.

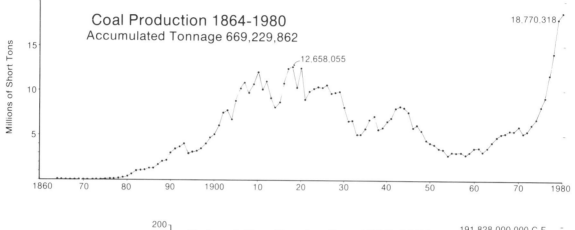

Coal Production 1864-1980
Accumulated Tonnage 669,229,862

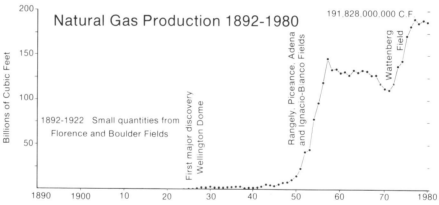

Natural Gas Production 1892-1980

oil, and natural gas (Table 1). Three counties in the Uravan Mineral Belt, Mesa, Montrose, and San Miguel, produce 80% of the uranium from more than 100 small carnotite mines in the relatively inaccessible canyons and mesas of the Colorado Plateau. Most of the remainder comes from large operations such as the Schwarzwalder Mine in Jefferson County and the Pitch Mine in Saguache County. Colorado continues as a major source of the strategic mineral that is refined into uranium oxide (U_3O_8) for energy and defense industries.

Non-metallic minerals comprise only a small proportion (7%) of production value. Characteristically of great bulk and low value, they are extracted from pits and quar-ries near their markets. These raw mate-rials — sand, gravel, clay, stone, and lime-stone — are washed, baked, trimmed, crushed or roasted for the construction trades. Not too surprisingly, counties with substantial population growth such as those in the Front Range Corridor, or those with interstate highway projects such as Eagle or with cement plants such as Larimer, Boulder, and Fremont Counties are major sources of build-ing materials. In the past, uncontrolled ex-traction of sand, gravel, and stone from floodplains and foothills has pocked and pitted thousands of acres in our most densely populated locales. Recently, however, in-creasing competition between cities and counties and the mining companies has led to better, but not necessarily ideal reclama-tion practices.

Colorado was born of and nurtured by the minerals industry. As suggested earlier, it attracted settlers, spawned the cities, fostered agriculture, manufacturing, and transporta-tion, and dominated the economy until the turn of the century. Although subsequently relegated to a lower rung on the economic ladder, mining remains a significant provider of raw materials, employment, and revenues. With the increasing demand for fossil fuels, alloy minerals, and construction materials, the future appears bright. Future optimism and actions, however, must be tempered by reality — 120 years of boom-bust cycles for each and every mineral.

Coal Bearing Regions, Fields, and Mines: 1980

GREEN RIVER
North Park
NORTH PARK
Yampa
Danforth Hills
UINTA
South Park
DENVER
Book Cliffs
Carbondale
Somerset
Note: Total Production was 18.8 million tons with 70% from 24 strip mines and 30% from 32 underground mines.
Colorado Springs Field
Canon City
Nucla Naturita
Bayfield
Yellowjacket
Walsenburg
Durango
RATON MESA
Trinidad
SAN JUAN RIVER

☐ Coal-bearing region

⊡ Producing fields
Strip mine
Underground mine

Petroleum and Natural Gas Provinces

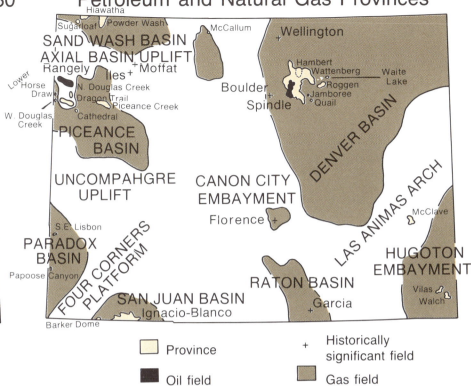

Hiawatha
Sugarloaf
Powder Wash
McCallum
Wellington
SAND WASH BASIN
AXIAL BASIN UPLIFT
Hambert Wattenberg Waite Lake
Rangely
Iles
Moffat
Roggen
Lower Horse Draw
N. Douglas Creek
Boulder
Jamboree
Dragon Trail
Spindle
Quail
W. Douglas Creek
Cathedral
Piceance Creek
PICEANCE BASIN
DENVER BASIN
UNCOMPAHGRE UPLIFT
CANON CITY EMBAYMENT
LAS ANIMAS ARCH
McClave
Florence
S.E. Lisbon
PARADOX BASIN
HUGOTON EMBAYMENT
Papoose Canyon
FOUR CORNERS PLATFORM
RATON BASIN
Vilas
Walch
SAN JUAN BASIN
Ignacio-Blanco
Garcia
Barker Dome

☐ Province
✛ Historically significant field
■ Oil field
▨ Gas field

Oil Shale Deposits

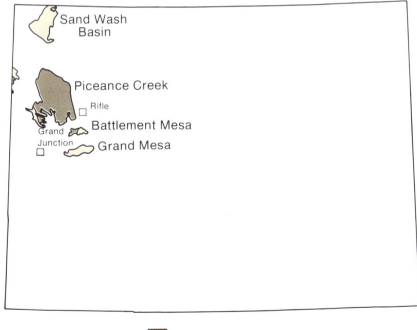

Sand Wash Basin
Piceance Creek
Rifle
Battlement Mesa
Grand Junction
Grand Mesa

▨ High yield shales (>25 gal. oil/ton)

☐ Shales of lesser potential

FOSSIL FUELS
Major Producing Areas

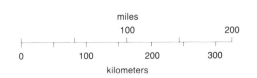

miles
0   100   200
0   100   200   300
kilometers

Indians of Colorado

PREHISTORY AND HISTORY. More than 10,000 years before the first European explorer arrived in Colorado, human beings had established themselves within what are now the present boundaries. Around 9,000 B.C., on the eastern plains of Colorado near modern Dent, groups of early Coloradans killed huge mammoths with specialized stone projectile points mounted on spears. Although human occupation in Colorado may go back more than 12,000 years, the Dent site currently marks the earliest archeological site discovered within the state.

These earliest known inhabitants of Colorado are called Paleoindians, or Big Game hunters, of the eastern plains. On the western plateaus, people of a similar culture existed with limited access to the larger game animals. It is unlikely that any of these early Coloradans resided permanently in the higher mountains; yet people from the plains and plateaus frequently entered the highlands in search of wood, stone, and food. The Paleoindians are best known for their specialized hunting of the larger herds of migratory animals such as the bison, mammoth, and mastodon and for the culture that depended on these animals. Lacking the larger animals, the people of the drier western plateaus hunted such small game as deer and rabbits and foraged on the native vegetation and insects.

By 8,500 B.C. many of the larger mammals in Colorado had become extinct, prompting the Paleoindians to rely more exclusively on smaller game and native vegetation, develop stone tools for grinding vegetation, and refine their small game hunting and trapping technology. The climate, formerly wet and cold, generally and gradually became warmer and drier, and by 3,000–2,000 B.C. closely resembled the present climate. The peoples of both the western plateaus and the eastern plains lived at subsistence levels, populations at times barely clinging to their meager existences.

Sometime before the birth of Christ, horticulture arrived in southwestern Colorado and the eastern plains, causing major social and economic changes, such as the use of pottery as a form of storage for grains. The Fremont people developed in Utah and the western one-third of Colorado and introduced horticultural practices, well-developed basketry, crude pottery, and small family dwellings.

The Anasazi, probably the best known of Colorado's early inhabitants, lived in the southwestern corner of the state. Before 500 A.D. the predecessors of the Anasazi lived as hunters and gatherers. The adoption of horticultural practices by circa 500 A.D. led to a more complex culture that featured small villages and half-underground family pithouses. Around 750 A.D. pottery was introduced and the village society continued to grow, reaching a zenith from about 1100 to 1300 A.D. During this high point the Anasazi constructed remarkably large villages such as the now-famous cliff dwellings at Mesa Verde.

By 1300 A.D. most of the Anasazi had left their homes on and around Mesa Verde, apparently forced out by prolonged drought, local depletion of natural resources, and human conflict. The Fremont people also vanished from our archeological view at this same time for unknown, but probably similar, reasons. On the eastern plains, small groups of Indians continued to live at subsistence levels.

When the Euro-Americans were first exploring Colorado in the sixteenth century, Indians of the state were almost all foragers with only a modest involvement with agriculture. From sometime before 1700 the Utes lived as hunters and gatherers in the mountains and western plateaus. The Apaches entered Colorado from the north and survived on nomadic hunting and limited horticulture on the eastern plains. The Shoshones and their relatives the Comanches hunted game north of the Yampa River in the northwestern corner of the state. In 1680, the Utes obtained horses when the Spanish were expelled from New Mexico during the Pueblo revolt. Horsemanship diffused from the Utes to the Comanches who with the acquisition

of horses pressed the Apaches ever southward.

The adoption of the horse also brought about new alignments of territory and entries of several tribes onto the Colorado plains in the eighteenth and nineteenth centuries. The Utes remained primarily in the mountain and plateau country but occasionally rode east in search of game. The Comanches roamed the high plains from Colorado to Mexico in the mid-1700s, finally settling in Oklahoma, Texas, and Mexico. The Kiowas formed an alliance with the Comanches in 1790 and travelled with them between the Arkansas River and Mexico. The Cheyenne, formerly sedentary agriculturalists from Minnesota, arrived in Colorado by the early 1800s. The Arapaho, hunters from Canada, joined the Cheyenne and lived as their allies on the eastern plains. Other tribes including the Navajo, Jicarilla Apache, Pawnee, and Sioux often conducted warring sojourns into Colorado.

By the early 1850s, treaties with the United States had been signed by most of the Colorado Indian tribes in order to reduce warring among various Indian factions. Later treaties sought to secure free and safe passage of travellers along the major trails through Colorado and generally allowed the Indians to remain in their traditional territories. However, by the late 1850s, American Indian policy had changed. Subsequent treaties would attempt to obtain more land for white settlers and to assign smaller fixed reservations to the Indians.

Starting in 1861 and ending in 1880, Colorado Indian tribes ceded huge parcels of land to the United States. Although neither Indians nor American frontiersmen honored the boundaries of these cessions, leading to frequent bloody clashes, the treaties did function to abruptly diminish the amount of land legally available to the Indians. With the final forced cession of land by the Utes in 1880, all of the land in Colorado had been taken from the Indians except for a small Ute reservation in the southwest corner. The Shoshones, Arapahoes, Cheyennes, Comanches, and Kiowas had been forced out of Colorado and onto government reservations in other states.

INDIAN TERRITORY BEFORE 1700

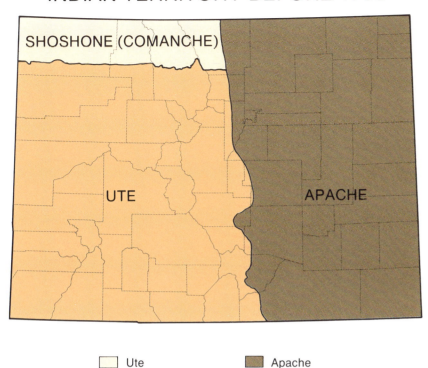

SHOSHONE (COMANCHE)

UTE

APACHE

☐ Ute   ☐ Apache

☐ Shoshone

INDIAN LAND CESSION TO THE UNITED STATES 1861-1880

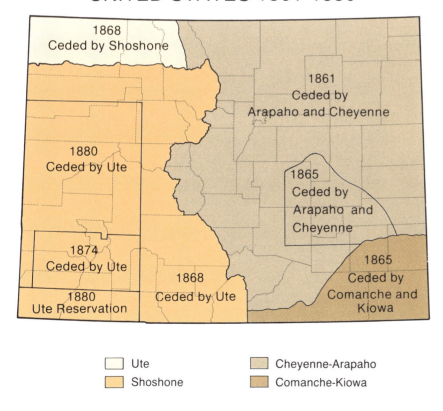

1868
Ceded by Shoshone

1861
Ceded by
Arapaho and Cheyenne

1880
Ceded by Ute

1865
Ceded by
Arapaho and
Cheyenne

1874
Ceded by Ute

1868
Ceded by Ute

1865
Ceded by
Comanche and
Kiowa

1880
Ute Reservation

☐ Ute   ☐ Cheyenne-Arapaho

☐ Shoshone   ☐ Comanche-Kiowa

CHRONOLOGICAL INDIAN DISTRIBUTION IN COLORADO

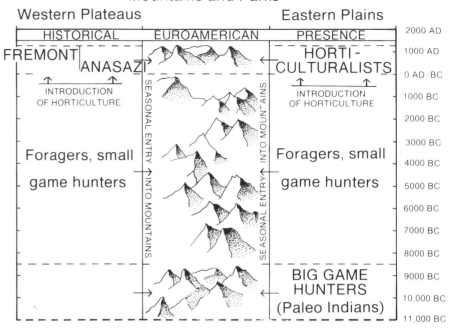

Mountains and Parks

Western Plateaus   Eastern Plains

| HISTORICAL | EUROAMERICAN | PRESENCE |

FREMONT ANASAZI   HORTI-CULTURALISTS

INTRODUCTION OF HORTICULTURE   INTRODUCTION OF HORTICULTURE

Foragers, small game hunters   Foragers, small game hunters

SEASONAL ENTRY INTO MOUNTAINS

SEASONAL ENTRY INTO MOUNTAINS

BIG GAME HUNTERS (Paleo Indians)

2000 AD
1000 AD
0 AD / BC
1000 BC
2000 BC
3000 BC
4000 BC
5000 BC
6000 BC
7000 BC
8000 BC
9000 BC
10,000 BC
11,000 BC

Modified from a diagram in Bruce E. Rippeteau's *A Colorado Book of the Dead,* Colorado State Historical Society, 1978.

Because Indians did not define fixed boundaries for their lands, all boundaries before 1861 are theoretical and therefore approximate.

Sources: Royce, Charles C. Indian Land Cession in the United States. Bureau of Ethnology Annual Report (1897).

INDIAN LANDS

miles
0   100   200

0   100   200   300
kilometers

Native Population Distribution circa 1500. The facing map has a two-fold purpose. First, it is designed to supplement the previous general discussion of Indian history in Colorado and to give a basic impression of the relative concentrations and approximate distributions of American Indians prior to the advent of the Europeans. Secondly, it distinguishes the adaptive systems that represented their primary means of support in somewhat restrictive environments of the semiarid plains and plateaus and the mountainous tracts of Colorado and adjoining states.

Basically, the Indians developed two adaptive systems for their subsistence—foraging and agriculture. However, few tribes probably depended exclusively on a single system for their domestic needs. Foraging is the periodic act of engaging in one or more of the following pursuits: collecting, hunting, or fishing to provide food, clothing, shelter, and implements. Indians who depended primarily on foraging were generally nomadic, made relatively little impact on the environment, and left few clues as to their exact numbers and their territorial range.

The Plains Indians followed the buffalo herds, hunting large and small game, and collecting seeds, fruit, and other food. During the wetter periods (normally late spring and summer) it was possible to live on the interfluves, since water was usually available within a day's journey. During dry periods and in winter the plains were essentially uninhabitable; thus the foragers concentrated along the riverine forests, in the mountain piedmonts, or on the tall grass prairies far to the east. Here they found shelter, fuel, and water, and from these bases sent hunting parties onto the open plains for food. Several large riverine cottonwood forests supported dense winter populations and annually provided this periodic protection. Since the foragers were less nomadic during the severe winters on the plains, the distributions shown represent winter encampments.

Finally, those foraging peoples who lived near the humid mountain "islands" engaged in a form of seasonal migration, moving into successively higher elevations as the snows retreated and utilizing the floral and faunal resources of the montane, subalpine, and alpine ecosystems as they became available. Such seasonal migration was particularly common in those portions of the state where summer temperatures were excessively hot.

Agriculturalists existed in surprisingly large numbers in the river valleys of the Great Plains and Southwest where they lived in permanent villages that occasionally contained hundreds of people if yields were large. In Colorado the plains farmers lived only in the very northeast corner, near today's Julesburg. Normally, the villages were along streams, but not necessarily large rivers since smaller ones could be more easily managed. Crops were raised in the seasonally created alluvia of stream beds and nurtured by underground water supplemented by whatever precipitation fell during the growing season. Corn, beans, and squash provided the dietary essentials, except for meat obtained on hunting forays. In the southwestern quadrant of Colorado along the tributaries of the Rio Grande and Colorado River, dams were usually built across small streams to create shallow pools and level alluvia in which crops were planted. Terracing was also fairly common, a practice designed to trap runoff, conserve soil, and provide level tiers for intensive use of hilly terrain.

In addition to the traditional growing of crops in or near the stream beds, irrigation agriculture was developed hundreds of years before the arrival of the Spanish. The most famous, extensive, and sophisticated systems for the diversion and delivery of water were constructed in the Salt and Gila valleys of Arizona. Elsewhere, in southwesternmost Colorado and in adjacent Arizona and New Mexico, most large pueblos also relied on irrigation, but not to the same degree. Food surpluses permitted the evolution of a highly specialized and structured society with considerable leisure time for the development of art, handicrafts, and architecture. The map shows the period of greatest development of irrigation agriculture between the tenth and thirteenth centuries. By 1400, most of the large settlements had been abandoned possibly because of drought, disease, increased soil salinity, or pressure from outside groups.

With some exceptions, American Indians exerted relatively little pressure on the so-called "fragile" environments of the state. First, they were few in number. A rough approximation suggests that fewer than 10,000 were dispersed over the 100,000 square miles of Colorado. At present, a smaller city such as Durango has substantially greater population within its city limits. Second, their demands on the environment were exceedingly small, with local mineral, vegetable, and animal resources providing life's essentials. With the possible exception of intentional burning of grasslands, or the occasional overkill of buffalo, theirs was a relatively harmonious relationship with the harsh environments of Colorado. The advent of the Europeans, with different demands and attitudes, initiated a process of environmental modification that has accelerated with the passage of time.

SELECTED REFERENCES

Goddard, P. E. *Indians of the Southwest* (New York: American Museum of Natural History, 1921).

Kroeber, A. L. *Cultural and Natural Areas of North America* (Berkeley: University of California Press, 1963).

Martin, P. S. and Quimby, Collier. *Indians Before Columbus* (Chicago: University of Chicago Press, 1947).

Wedel, W. R. "The High Plains and their Utilization by the Indian," *American Antiquity*, 29 (July 1963): 1–17.

Wormington, H. M. "Prehistoric Indians of the Southwest," Popular Series No. 7, Colorado Museum of Natural History, 1947.

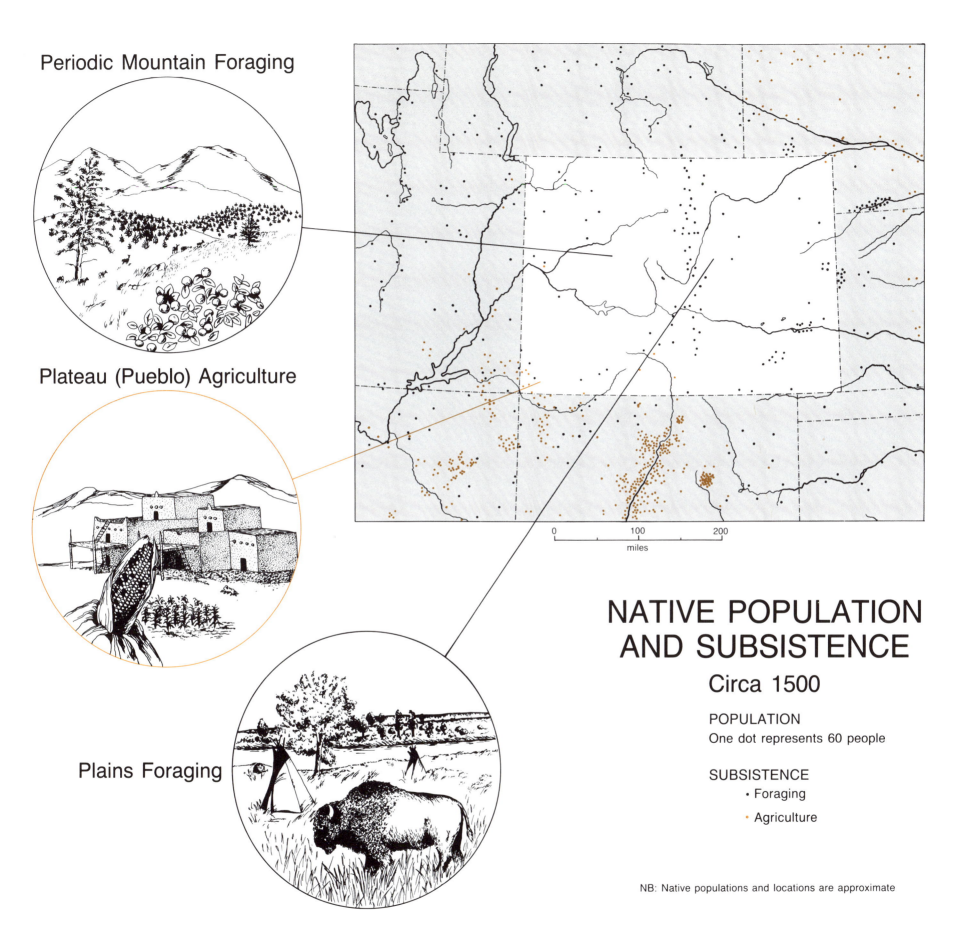

Periodic Mountain Foraging

Plateau (Pueblo) Agriculture

Plains Foraging

NATIVE POPULATION AND SUBSISTENCE

Circa 1500

POPULATION
One dot represents 60 people

SUBSISTENCE
- • Foraging
- • Agriculture

0   100   200
miles

NB: Native populations and locations are approximate

Early Exploration

THE YEAR 1850 marks the end of the period of early exploration in Colorado. After mid-century, at which time the rudimentary physical outlines were known, the numerous gold-seekers added to local knowledge and around 1870 the scientific surveys of the West officially described and mapped Colorado's major features.

Prior to 1850 at least 25 parties of record penetrated the area of modern Colorado in addition to the unrecorded explorations of fur trappers. These early explorers entered the unknown Colorado area from two directions: 1.) from the south along the Rio Grande or overland from Santa Fe following the Old Spanish Trail; and 2.) from the east up the South Platte and Arkansas from the Mississippi.

The earliest exploration activity emanated from Santa Fe and Taos in New Mexico. Among these notable Spanish parties are Humaña (1593), Ulibarri (1706), Valverde (1714), Villasur (1720), Rivera (1765), Vial (1793), and Serracino (1811). The record of the earliest explorers remained vague and indecisive until Padre Silvestre Velez de Escalante (1776), the most famous of the early Spanish explorers. Accompanied by Father Dominguez and 12 companions, Escalante left Santa Fe to establish a new route to California. On the first leg he followed the Old Spanish Trail into southwestern Colorado and from there wound northward, skirting the high ranges and crossing in succession the Dolores, Uncompahgre, Gunnison, and Colorado rivers to finally reach the White River near the present Utah border in northwestern Colorado. Thwarted in his effort to reach California, he turned back to Utah, recrossing the Colorado River and returning across northern Arizona and New Mexico. In the process of this epic journey, he saw more of the Southwest than any European before him. In Colorado, the Escalante traverse gave rough lineations of ranges and rivers and provided important descriptive information, such as the finding of the Anasazi ruins near what is today Dolores, Colorado.

The thrust from the east came originally from American fur trappers, many of French extraction. Following rivers up from the Mississippi into the Rockies, the great surge of "mountain men" reached Colorado via the Platte and Arkansas around 1800, although the Mallet brothers (1739) provide an early exception. The record during the fur trading period is truly scanty. Williams (1811) and Bell (1819) give accounts of the Front Range area and Arkansas valley. Later, in the 1820s, as a Taos–Salt Lake trading axis evolved, American explorers such as Lieutenant Zebulon Pike and Major Stephen Long provided sketchy accounts of the area that was to become Colorado.

Pike and 22 men left St. Louis in July, 1806, with orders to conclude Indian treaties and to explore the headwaters of the Arkansas River. The small expedition followed the Arkansas upstream to the site of modern Pueblo, Colorado, where Pike established a camp as a base from which he and three men marched northwestward to ascend the peak that now bears his name. Proceeding upriver, the party encountered Royal Gorge, detoured northward up into South Park, dropped down into the Upper Arkansas, followed the river northward nearly to the site of present Leadville. Returning back through South Park, Pike set out southward with a party of 14 in a fruitless search for the headwaters of the Red River. This quest brought him into the San Luis Valley, the Rio Grande drainage, and into the hands of 100 Spanish troops. Arrested and taken to Chihuahua, Mexico, Pike was officially deported to the United States after a confinement of several months.

Major Long's expedition, scientific in scope, entered Colorado in 1820 from the Missouri valley to the north. A small group (20 men) followed the Platte River and reached the future site of Denver in July and Manitou Springs a week later where Dr. James, the party's naturalist, climbed Pikes Peak and recorded finds of plants and animals of the tundra. The party split at the Arkansas River, one group returning downstream and the other, under Long, trekking south and overland in another vain attempt to reach the headwaters of the Red River. After considerable trials, Long returned to Fort Smith, Arkansas, in September.

The closing period of early exploration, 1835–1850, was marked by variations on established trails and routes. Notable in the period were Abert, Wyeth, Childes, and Kearny, but best known was John C. Frémont, whose vision of manifest destiny was typified in the war with Mexico in the mid-1840s. The Frémont expeditions basically involved east–west crossings of Colorado from Independence, Missouri, to California and Oregon and back. In 1843 he followed the South Platte to Fort St. Vrain (route not shown) and north to the Oregon Trail. On his return from California in 1844 he traversed Colorado from west to east, from the Colorado drainage in the northwest, up the Blue River, over into South Park, and down the Arkansas. Returning to the West Coast the following year, Frémont retraced the route up the Arkansas, then crossed the Continental Divide west of the Gore Range and moving northward struck the source of the White River near Trappers Lake.

The great scientific surveys of the 1870s — Wheeler, Powell, and especially Hayden — concluded the era of early exploration.

SELECTED REFERENCES

Chittenden, Hiram M. *The American Fur Trade of the Far West.* 2 vols. (Stanford: Academic Reprints, 1954).

Goetzmann, William. *Exploration and Empire* (New York: Alfred Knopf, 1966).

Hafen, Leroy R. and Ann W. Hafen (eds.). *Far West and Rockies Series.* 15 vols. (Glendale, California: Arthur H. Clark Co., 1954-61).

Hafen, Leroy R. and Carl Coke Rister. *Western America* (New York: Prentice-Hall, 1950).

EARLY EXPLORATION
Selected Routes

—·—·—·—·—· Escalante 1776

·················· Pike 1806

— — — — — Long 1820

——————— Frémont 1844

━━━━━━━ Frémont 1845

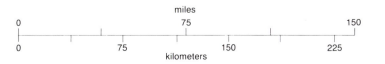

miles

0   75   150

0   75   150   225

kilometers

Population Distribution

CENSUS WORKERS IN 1980 counted 2,889,964 persons residing within the state's land area of 103,766 square miles.[1] The population density of the state, at best a crude measure, thus becomes approximately 28 persons per square mile (p/sm). By comparison, the Colorado figure of 28 p/sm stands substantially below the national average of 65 p/sm and slightly above the combined figure for the mountain states of 25 p/sm. In area, population numbers, and population density the state of Oregon is virtually the same as Colorado.

Within Colorado the population takes on a very uneven distribution so that a statewide density figure of 28 p/sm may be somewhat misleading. Some mountainous tracts may be totally devoid of a resident population; only a few families can be found over extensive ranching areas of both the eastern plains and western plateaus. Census figures indicate the unevenness. Of Colorado's 63 counties, 53 contain about 85% of the land area but only 19% of the population. Hinsdale County in the San Juan Mountains of southwestern Colorado could muster only 408 residents for the 1980 census. Eighty-five percent of Colorado has a population density of about 6 p/sm, a figure similar to the sister Rocky Mountain states of Wyoming and Montana. The corollary must be that the ten other counties are heavily populated.

Colorado is then "two" states: a large one of 53 low-density counties, typical of the mountain states; and the smaller 10-county state, densely populated, intensively cultivated, and strongly urban and industrial. The latter is the Front Range urban corridor of 10 counties whose population density exceeds 148 p/sm and bears more of a resemblance to a Midwestern agro-industrial state such as Indiana, than to the Rockies. The string of counties (Larimer, Weld, Boulder, Jefferson,

[1]This figure represents the total land area of counties only.

Adams, Arapahoe, Denver, Douglas, El Paso, and Pueblo) from the Wyoming border southward along the eastern edge of the Rockies in 1980 counted 2,326,479 persons, thus leaving only 563,485 scattered over the remainder of the state. Of the 2.3 million in the Front Range corridor, over 2 million are urban dwellers, or 90% of the 10-county strip (Table 1).

Table 1. FRONT RANGE COUNTIES

	Land Area (Square mi.)	Total Population	Urban Population
Adams	1,237	245,944	235,571
Arapahoe	797	293,621	286,197
Boulder	748	189,625	158,539
Denver	95	492,365	492,365
Douglas	843	25,153	4,070
El Paso	2,157	309,424	288,929
Jefferson	783	371,753	342,541
Larimer	2,611	149,184	110,987
Pueblo	2,405	125,972	109,490
Weld	4,002	123,438	70,784
	15,678	2,326,479	2,099,473

Although the urbanized corridor is the most striking feature of population distribution, a dot map reveals a number of characteristic patterns. One of these is the distinctive point clustering of population in nearly every county. Predictably, the clusters represent county seats which serve the administrative, educational, medical, and commercial needs of low population counties. These places tend to have between 2,000 and 10,000 people and appear as tiny collections of dots scattered across the map of Colorado.

The notable linear patterning of dots reflects the orientation of river valleys and major transportation axes, particularly national highways. Three river valleys may be singled out for their distinctive linear concentrations of population: 1.) the Platte Valley lineation which stretches from Denver to Sedgwick County in the northeastern corner of the state, a line reinforced by a similar alignment of Interstate 76; 2.) the lower Arkansas Valley, producing a regular line of dots from Pueblo across southeastern Colorado to the Kansas border and once again

paralleled by a major highway (U.S. 50); and 3.) the Colorado–Gunnison valley lines, notably east and west of Grand Junction and the fine trace of dots along the upper Colorado, etched along a portion of the line by Interstate 70. These three valleys tend to constrict irrigation agriculture, transportation route ways, and farms and small towns which produce the line patterns of the map. Away from the valleys two east–west linear patterns appear on the high plains of eastern Colorado, both lines of major highways (U.S. 34 and I-70).

Finally, the population distribution pattern shows two broadly consolidated areas of rural and small town residence. One of these rather densely populated areas is the Colorado piedmont lying within the Front Range corridor. From Table 1 it is apparent that over 200,000 people within the urbanized corridor live on farms or in places with less than 2,500 inhabitants. They constitute the non-urban piedmont population settled across a rich, irrigated farm landscape that owes its existence to nearby mountain waters, diverted and impounded for crops in the broad longitudinal zone between Denver and Fort Collins. The second broadly consolidated population area is found in the San Luis Valley, another large irrigated region in parts of Conejos, Rio Grande, Alamosa, and Saguache counties where the combined population of nearly 30,000 is 78% rural.

Population Change 1910–1980. A cursory look at seven decades of population change reveals an almost complete reversal of growth patterns. Early population figures indicate strong growth in the eastern counties and marked decline in the mountain counties of western Colorado. The most recent census (1980) shows decennial losses of population in the east (13 counties with absolute population loss) and pronounced growth in the west, particularly the mountain counties. Denver and its adjacent counties form an exception to the general pattern shift in that the Denver area displayed rather strong and sustained growth throughout the 70 years from 1910.

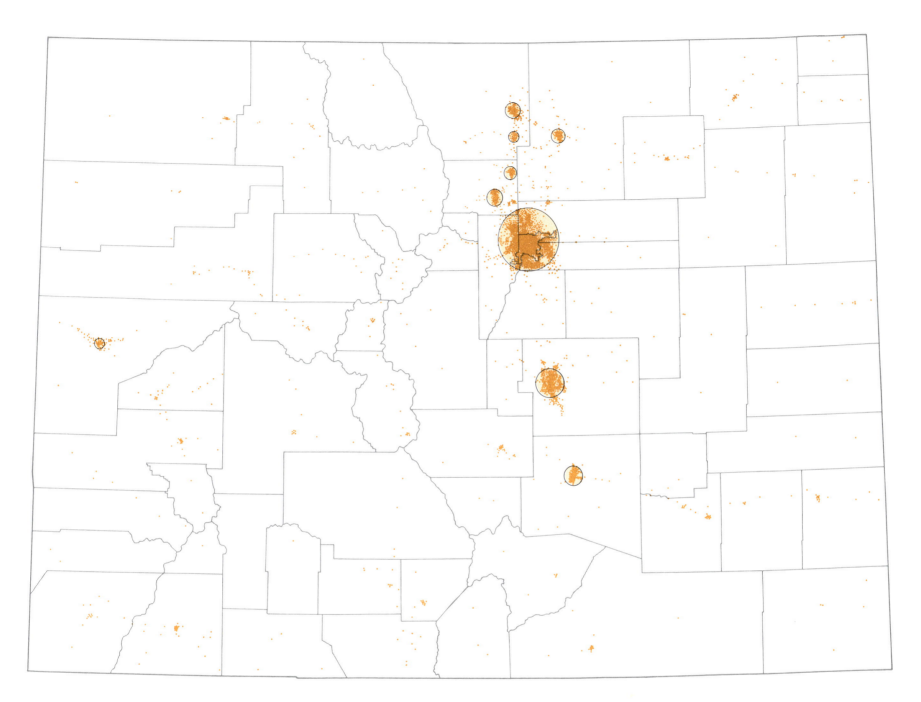

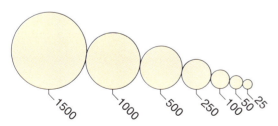

Urban Population in Thousands of Persons

1500 1000 500 250 100 50 25

POPULATION DISTRIBUTION
1980

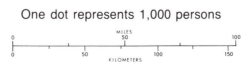

One dot represents 1,000 persons

Source: U.S. Census of Population, 1980

MILES
0 50 100

KILOMETERS
0 50 100 150

1910–1920

The map of this decade catches the final push of settlers into the last reaches of the Great Plains, i.e., Colorado, the whole band of eastern counties stretching from the Wyoming border to the New Mexico–Oklahoma line. Newly plowed soils, a series of wetter years, mechanization, and good grain prices encouraged the dry farming of wheat, a boom that peaked around 1917. In contrast, the earlier mining boom had gone bust and, as the map illustrates, the mountain counties lost population, Gilpin and Teller counties losing over half their number in just 10 years.

1920–1930

The roaring twenties did not roar so loudly in Colorado. After World War I livestock and grain prices fell over 50% and brought about increasing foreclosure and tenancy. A number of counties in the east, which only a decade before had boasted population growth of 25% or more, now lost people. The mining industry's wartime metallics production (gold, copper, zinc, tungsten, lead, and vanadium) failed from too little demand and too much foreign competition. The mining slowdown translates directly into substantial population losses in two traditional mining areas: 1.) the central area of Teller, Clear Creek, Summit, Lake, and Pitkin counties; and 2.) the San Juan area, notably San Miguel and Ouray counties. Growth around Denver reflects the emergence of the High Plains wholesaling and retailing center and peripheral expansion encouraged by interurban railroads and expanded by the automobile. The second growth center (Saguache-Rio Grande-Alamosa) in the San Luis Valley displays the impact of newly organized irrigation agriculture and specialty cropping (McClure red potatoes and sugar beets).

1930–1940

The population decline of eastern Colorado counties vividly delineates the collapse of the agricultural economy of the High Plains. Depression and drought, epitomized by the popularized "Dust Bowl," brought about absolute decline in 19 eastern counties, three in the southeast showing losses over 25% in the 10-year nadir. A fixed gold price and new metal demands revitalized the mountain counties during the same decade and produced the yoyo-like return of growth over 25% to counties that showed over 25% losses in the previous decade: Clear Creek, Teller, Summit, and San Miguel.

1940–1950

Population losses became more widespread during the 1940s and dispelled the notion that the Depression ended with World War II. The mountain counties once more produced a mass exodus of population and a number of plains counties, particularly the northeastern, continued the absolute losses that began in the 1920s. A major petroleum development (Rangely Field in Rio Blanco County) and limited urban growth, some associated with military development, break the pattern of loss.

1950–1960

The rather surprising population decline of the 1950s outstripped the county losses of the Depression and the 1940s: more failing counties, widespread decline and stagnation, and numerous deep population losses in the range of 10–30%. Amid the overall decline, two notable growth patterns foreshadowed the characteristics of subsequent decades. First, urban growth in counties around Denver and Colorado Springs exceeded 25%, portending the emergence of an urbanized corridor just east of the Front Range. Second, the conspicuous growth of Summit (83% increase) and Pitkin (45% increase) counties signalled a nascent resurgence in the high country and an economy heavily dependent on skiing, water development, and mountain resort and vacation home building. A minor increase shows up in the southwestern corner of the state and was associated primarily with uranium exploration and processing.

1960–1970

The pattern of gains and losses during the 1960s continues the trends established in the preceding decade. The Front Range corridor now included growing counties from the Wyoming border to El Paso County. The mountain counties proximate to the corridor also showed a modest growth reflecting urban recreational usage and transportation improvements. Thus the north–south strip of counties (Jackson to Fremont) reversed losses apparent in the 1950s. Pitkin County (Aspen) epitomized the recreation-dependent growth and became the fastest growing county during the decade with a 160% increase. The pattern of population loss continued for the fifth consecutive decade in many counties of the eastern plains. The short-lived uranium boom came to a sudden halt and was reflected in losses in the southwestern counties.

1970–1980

Coming up to the present, the decade of the 1970s produced a fulfillment of the pattern established in the 1950s: suburban growth in the Front Range corridor and mountain recreation expansion, the latter reinforced by energy development in the plateau country of northwestern Colorado (see p. 29). The suburban growth now takes on the classic features of the urban doughnut, the declining core and expanding periphery; and, albeit in a rough pattern, the City and County of Denver shows for the first time absolute loss amid growing counties on all sides. This peripheral expansion of population and industry agrees with the manufacturing decentralization of the last three decades (see p. 60). The unrelenting losses of population in eastern Colorado farming counties heighten the contrast of mountain and plain. Three low population plains counties have shown absolute population loss during every decade from the 1920s.

Minority Populations. Place names are important but imperfect reflections of an area's racial and ethnic composition with disproportionate shares added to the land by the original inhabitants and early settlers. Colorado is no exception to this generalization. Indian names, although linguistically fractured in translation, are relatively abundant and applied to mountains, rivers, and counties. Most places, however, bear Spanish or

1910-1920

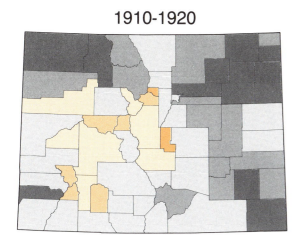

1920-1930

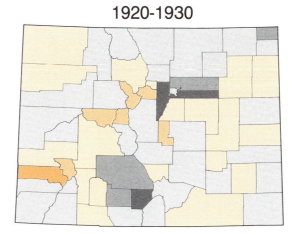

1930-1940

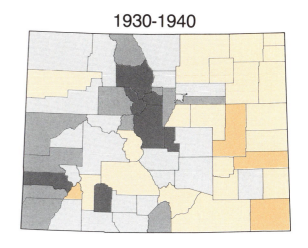

1940-1950

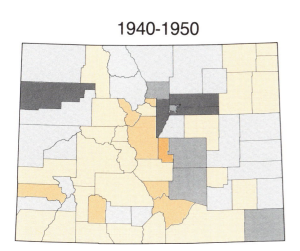

1950-1960

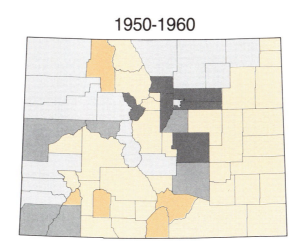

1960-1970

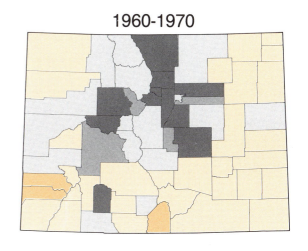

1970-1980

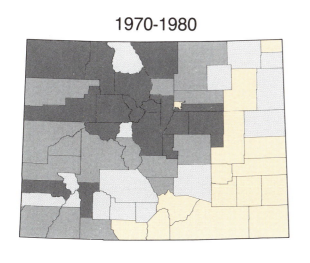

% Change

more than 50.0 gain

25.0 to 49.9 gain

0 to 24.9 gain

0. to 24.9 loss

25 to 49.9 loss

more than 50.0 loss

Source: U.S. Census of Population
1920 to 1980.

POPULATION
CHANGE
1910-1980

miles

| 0 | 100 | 200 | 300 |

| 0 | 100 | 200 | 300 | 400 | 500 |

kilometers

English (including American) names whose distribution clearly outlines respective spheres of influence in the early exploration and settlement of Colorado.

Individuals of European heritage now constitute approximately 95% of the state's population (Table 2). The majority arrived and settled in Colorado via Anglo-America but a significant minority with Spanish roots migrated northward from Latin America. Approximately 340,000 individuals, or 12% of Colorado's population, declared they were of Spanish origin (Chicano) in 1980. This group denoted either specific Spanish origin categories—Mexican, Puerto Rican, or Cuban—or reported "other Spanish/Hispanic" origins including Spain, or Spanish-speaking countries of Central or South America, or identified themselves generally as Spanish, Spanish-American, Hispano, Latino, or Chicano.

Maps of Hispanic distribution suggest significant patterns and concentrations. About half (50.5%) live in three counties (Denver, Pueblo, and Arapahoe) while the other half are dispersed in less urbanized counties (Map 1). This statewide distribution is more apparent when the proportion (rather than percentages of 340,000) of persons of Spanish origin of the total county population is plotted. In all but five counties 2% or more of the inhabitants are Chicano, and in those counties that once constituted the Spanish borderland 30 to 78% of the residents claim Spanish origin (Map 2). These colorfully and distinctively named counties—Archuleta, Saguache, Rio Grande, Alamosa, Conejos, Costilla, Pueblo, Otero, Huerfano, and Las Animas—are essentially the same as those in which Spanish is spoken in a large propor-tion (14% to more than 28%) of the households (Map 3). In Costilla 76% of households speak Spanish at home.

Although these southern counties are the cradle of Spanish culture in Colorado, their population is largely rural, agricultural, and numerically small. Larger numbers live where they or their parents were initially recruited as contract laborers for long hours and low pay in the irrigated valleys of the North Platte and Arkansas rivers. Others performed equally onerous tasks as unskilled workers in the iron and steel mills of Pueblo or in the smelters and mines of Leadville. Increasing mechanization of agriculture, especially in sugar beet cultivation and harvesting, reduced the demand for field workers and many moved to Denver, Greeley, and other piedmont cities in search of a better life. Their descendants and new migrants (including illegal aliens) concentrate in the Spanish districts of the urban centers, especially in central Denver along the Platte River.

Blacks, Asians, and American Indians constitute smaller but significant minorities (Table 2). All three groups tend to be more concentrated or localized than persons of Spanish origin. For example, 97.3% of Blacks live in only 7 counties; 95.6% of Asians reside in 10 counties; and 88.9% of Indians dwell in 13 counties (Table 3).

Blacks include those who reported their race as Black or Negro or who identified themselves as Jamaican, Black Puerto Rican, Haitian, or Nigerian. They are primarily urban dwellers living only in appreciable numbers in those counties that constitute Colorado's three metropolitan areas. An astonishing 58% live in the City and County of Denver with further localization in such districts as Five Points and Park Hill.

Asians and Pacific Islanders include those persons who specifically indicated their race as Japanese, Chinese, Filipino, Korean, Vietnamese, Asian, Indian, Hawaiian, Guamanian, Samoan, and others who entered such terms as Cambodian, Laotian, Pakistani, and Fiji Islanders. This minority of 34,257 is clustered in the same seven counties as the Blacks, plus Larimer, Weld, and Mesa. Unlike Blacks, only 26% of Asians reside in

Table 3. DISTRIBUTION OF MINORITIES*
% of totals by counties

County	Blacks 101,695	Asians 34,257	Indians 21,015
Denver	58.1	26.1	20.6
El Paso	18.8	15.7	9.8
Arapahoe	8.3	13.4	7.1
Adams	6.1	10.8	10.0
Pueblo	2.4	1.7	3.7
Jefferson	1.9	12.9	8.8
Boulder	1.7	7.2	4.4
Larimer	—	4.3	4.9
Weld	—	2.6	2.5
Mesa	—	1.2	2.9
Montezuma	—	—	7.6
La Plata	—	—	5.4
Fremont	—	—	1.2
	97.3	95.9	88.9

*Only counties with 1% or more of a minority group are shown.

Denver with more than 44% in nearby suburban counties—Jefferson, Arapahoe, Adams, and Boulder. Also, a large proportion are relatively new arrivals who have fled war-ravaged countries of eastern and southeastern Asia in search of a new and better life.

The American Indian, Eskimo, and Aleut category makes up 0.7% of Colorado's population with its 21,015 individuals fairly well dispersed. Thirteen counties (Table 3) contain 89% of the total with the largest concentration in Denver (20.6%) and Adams (10.0%). The remaining three-fifths are spread throughout the Front Range corridor and three Western Slope counties. Those in eastern Colorado tend to be plains Indians especially from Nebraska, Wyoming, and the Dakotas who have difficulty adjusting to urban environments while those in the southwest (13% in Montezuma and La Plata Counties) are principally descendants from the once powerful Utes and Navajos.

Table 2. RACIAL/ETHNIC ELEMENTS
(approximate percentages*)

White	89.7
Spanish origin	11.8
Black	3.5
Asian	1.2
Indian	0.7

*These figures will not total 100%. Persons of Spanish origin may be of any race. Evidently, most declared they were white.

Spanish Spoken at Home

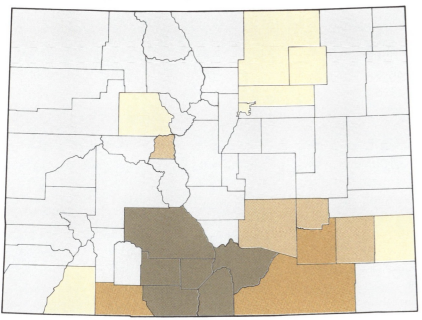

Percent of families speaking Spanish at home

☐ 0-6.9	☐ 21-27.9
☐ 7-13.9	☐ Over 28
☐ 14-20.9	

Hispanic Concentration

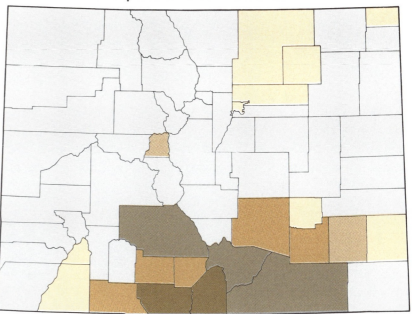

Proportion of population (co.) declaring Hispanic origin in percent

☐ 0-10	☐ 30-40
☐ 10-20	☐ 40-50
☐ 20-30	☐ Over 50

State percentage: 11.87

Statewide Hispanic Population

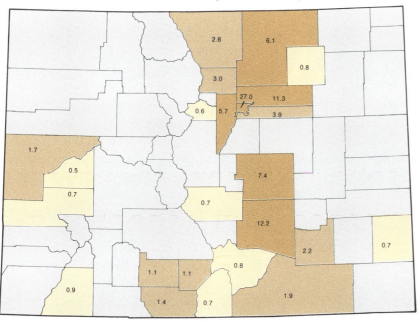

Proportion of population (state) declaring Hispanic origin in percent

☐ 0-.5	☐ 1.0-5.0
☐ .5-1.0	☐ Over 5.0

PEOPLE OF HISPANIC ORIGIN

Source: U.S. Census of Population, 1980

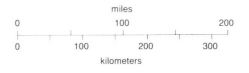

Housing Characteristics

BUILDINGS OF ALL sizes, shapes, and functions are conspicuous features of the landscape. Architecture not only reflects economic pursuits but also suggests degrees of affluence, life styles, and population densities. Houses, more numerous and more architecturally varied than other buildings, represent a particularly personal bond to the land. More than any other element on the landscape, they create impressions of what places are like, images that are colorfully and pointedly labeled, such as "condo counties," suburban fringes, or retirement villages. The accompanying maps, based on quantitative information in the 1980 Census of Population and Housing, selectively illustrate some of these characteristics specifically highlighting the distribution, age, and type of homes.

Age of Houses. The year 1940 is an appropriate dividing line in the age of housing. Those built before 1940 represent pre-World War II economic emphasis, particularly farming and mining, locational focus, and social function. In form, these houses generally fall under three basic types: 1.) the midwestern frame farmhouse and its variations, including the elaborate Victorian; 2.) the bungalow style; and 3.) for want of a better term, the cabin, a roughly finished one-story, rectangular shack built quickly with rustic materials. In addition to these three common types, the two or three-story "rooming house," ornate mansion architecture, and the true southwestern "rancho" of heavy frame and adobe construction may be locally significant in the housing mix.

Postwar houses reflect the increasing mobility, affluence, and industrial orientation of the state's population. The suburban housing boom produced seemingly endless repetitions of the frame rancho and its multistory and split-level variations. Many old frame farmhouses were replaced by the new rancho style, particularly with the succession and inheritance of subsequent generations and with consolidation in older farming areas and agricultural expansion into newly irrigated lands. Mobile homes, appearing singly in once marginal farming lands, or grouped in "parks" within booming suburbs or new growth points (such as near new energy finds), bear a resemblance to an earlier form if seen as an aluminum-clothed, long, rectangular, frame cabin. Postwar affluence also provided a second housing expansion, this time for recreation, into the mountains. This second surge gave rise to A-frame, chalet, and mine-shaft styles that typify the new mountain playgrounds.

As expected, the counties with 40% or more of their houses built before 1940 are the older settled farming and mining counties that have grown little since their economic heyday. An imaginary line drawn from the state's southwestern corner to the northeastern corner noticeably divides housing age into newer (upper left) and older (lower right) regions.

Second Homes. Census takers classify a housing unit as vacant if unoccupied at the time of enumeration. The vacant units are further classified into two groups: 1.) seasonal and migratory, which includes summer or winter houses, sports lodges, and residences occupied for specific times during the year; and 2.) year-round vacant, which includes a category "held for occasional use" in order to designate occasional weekend occupation, shared ownerships, and time-share condominiums. A combination of these groups provides a figure of total units that might be classed as second homes. The number of second homes as a percentage of housing units further refines the breakdown by assigning relative importance of second homes in each county.

The urban and agricultural counties contain relatively few second homes—indeed, their populations represent the second home owners. On the other hand, the higher categories (above 15%) sharply etch the mountain counties of Colorado except for a "lowland wedge" in the Upper Arkansas Valley counties of Fremont, Chaffee, and Lake.

Eleven counties have second home percentages greater than 25%: Jackson, Grand, Eagle, Gilpin, Summit, Pitkin, Park, Teller, Custer, Hinsdale, and Archuleta and three (Summit, Park, and Hinsdale) exceed 50%! Such high proportions bring into focus the "peak load" problem of vacation housing. Service personnel in the public sector must be maintained at a rather high and inefficient level for much of the year; public utilities require abnormally high capacities.

Mobile Homes. Modern technology's answer to housing scarcity and increasing construction costs is the mobile home, a recent phenomenon that transcends with uniformity the traditional regional distinctions of house types. As totally prefabricated units, they are "mobile" only in the sense of being shipped on wheeled carriages, but once set up on a housing sight, they become fixed structures that are expensive to relocate and are thus rarely moved. How long the mobile home will persist in the landscape is a moot question, but one would expect a long-time continuance, if for no other reason than growth trends in mobile home sales. In Colorado, mobile homes comprise 5.7% of total housing units, a figure climbing from 2.1% in 1960 and 4.0% in 1970.

The basic mobile home unit (12' × 64') and the double wide (24' × 49') provide a simple and inexpensive means to add between 800 to 1200 square feet for housing. The map reflects three basic uses for mobile homes: 1.) older farmstead conversions for remodeling, consolidation relocations, or accommodation of family generations; 2.) economic boom housing geared to low investment costs of younger, lower income families; and 3.) recreation second homes for middle income families which tend to emphasize the summer vacation in the mountains but away from posher ski resorts. These three demands, in fact, characterize many Colorado counties outside the urban corridor along the Front Range. Local municipal and county restrictions will also affect the percentage of some distributions.

Age of Houses

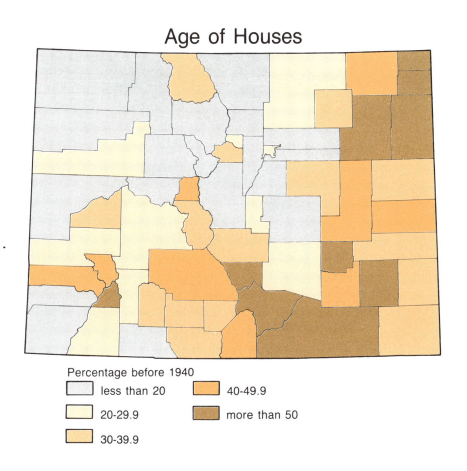

Percentage before 1940

- less than 20
- 20-29.9
- 30-39.9
- 40-49.9
- more than 50

Second Homes

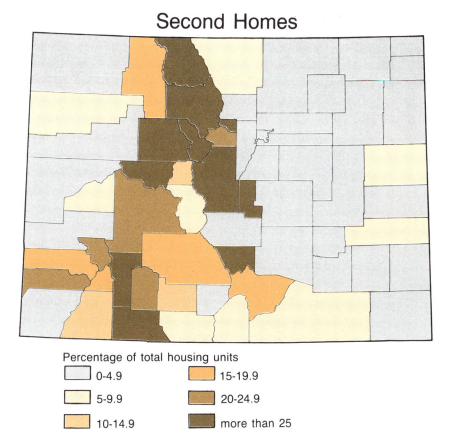

Percentage of total housing units

- 0-4.9
- 5-9.9
- 10-14.9
- 15-19.9
- 20-24.9
- more than 25

Mobile Homes

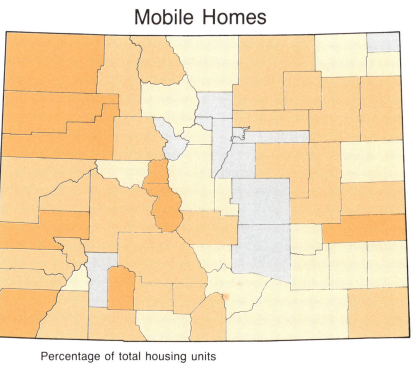

Percentage of total housing units

- less than 5
- 5.0-9.9
- 10.0-14.9
- more than 15

HOUSING CHARACTERISTICS
1980

Source: U.S. Census of Population and Housing, 1980

miles

0   100   200

0   100   200   300

kilometers

Income Distribution

Tʜᴇ ᴍᴀᴘs ᴏɴ the facing page utilize two rather common measures of income: median family income by county and percent of families below poverty level by county. The figures come from the 1980 Census of Population and reflect incomes gained in the last full year prior to the census, in this case 1979. One would expect an inverse relationship to exist between median family income and the percentage below poverty level—that counties with a high percentage of families below poverty level would also show a low median income or, stated in another fashion, as poverty increases the median income should decrease. A third map of "residuals of regression" indicates just how true that relationship is for each county.

Median Family Income. The median family income (MFI) for the state in 1980 was $21,280, meaning that exactly one-half of all families had incomes larger than this figure, and another half had incomes smaller. Generally, the northern and western counties show the higher family incomes, with particularly high MFIs noticeable for the rapidly growing Denver suburban counties (Douglas, Jefferson, and Arapahoe) and for two mountain recreation counties (Pitkin and Summit). MFI levels taper off sharply toward the southern and eastern farming counties with south-central Colorado showing the lowest MFIs.

Percent of Families Below Poverty Level. Census figures indicate that 7.4% of the state's families had incomes below poverty level, a line subject to much redefinition and adjustment. In establishing poverty thresholds for 1979, family size and age of householder entered into the definitions with an inflation adjustment based on the Consumer Price Index. The poverty thresholds shown below unfortunately reflect nationwide standards and are not adjusted for regional variations in the cost of living and dependence on subsistence agriculture.

Size of family	Threshold
1 person:	
Under 65 years	$ 3,774
65 years and over	3,479
2 persons:	
Householder under 65 years	4,876
Householder 65 years and over	4,389
3 persons	5,787
4 persons	7,412
5 persons	8,776
6 persons	9,915
7 persons	11,237
8 persons	12,484
9 or more persons	14,812

The pattern of counties with lower percentages of poverty correspond rather well to the previous pattern of high MFI counties and the same northwest–southeast slope toward greater poverty persists. All the counties surrounding Denver show poverty levels of 6% or less; Denver, the typical "hole-in-the-doughnut" of affluence, shows over 10% of families with incomes below the poverty level. At the time of the census, high employment rates in the energy extraction counties of northwestern Colorado produced a general affluence and poverty levels under 5%. The greatest family poverty in the state occurs in the southern San Luis Valley where Conejos and Costilla counties display family poverty percentages of 27.1 and 32.3, respectively.

Comparing the Maps. Close inspection of the two maps shows that poverty corresponds to low income—hardly a discovery, but how well do they correspond? Hypothetically, a county with a low median income of, say, $14,900 could have no families below poverty level, *if* the family incomes happened to be perfectly evenly distributed. Thus, how well counties on the two maps agree will say something about income distribution. For example, Hinsdale County in the southwestern part of the state stands out on one map for family poverty below 5% and on the other map for a low median family income, a lack of congruity that begs for quantification.

The dots on the scatter diagram below represent the 63 counties of the state, each plotted by poverty percentage (x axis) against median income (y axis). The pattern of dots (counties) generally shows a relationship between increasing income and decreasing poverty, statistically shown as a regression line roughly bisecting the scatter of dots. If all dots were located exactly on the line, as beads on a string, a perfect negative correlation (–1.00) would exist. The counties obviously vary around the regression line, but do show a definite tendency to follow the line and altogether produce a relatively high correlation coefficient (r) of –.82. The counties above the line have more poverty than predicted on the basis of income, those below have less poverty than incomes would indicate. The distances away from the line (above or below) are called *residuals of regression* and, in this case, are really income discrepancies which can be mapped. Two additional lines (statistically "one standard error," SE_y) may be drawn $2,500 above and below the central regression line to produce four categories for mapping the counties: above 1.0 SE_y; 0.0 to 1.0 SE_y; 0.0 to –1.0 SE_y; and below –1.0 SE_y.

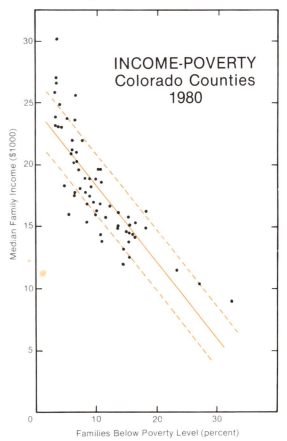

Median Family Income
State: $21,280

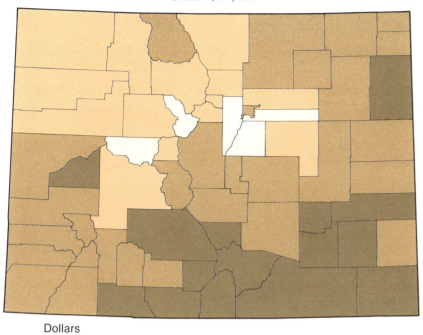

Dollars

- ▨ under 15,000
- ▨ 15,000-19,999
- ▨ 20,000-24,999
- ☐ Over 25,000

Percentage of Families Below Poverty
State: 7.4%

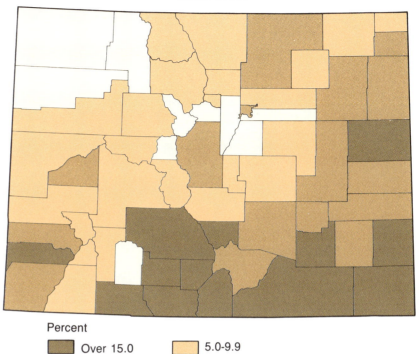

Percent

- ▨ Over 15.0
- ▨ 10.0-14.9
- ▨ 5.0-9.9
- ☐ under 5.0

Residuals

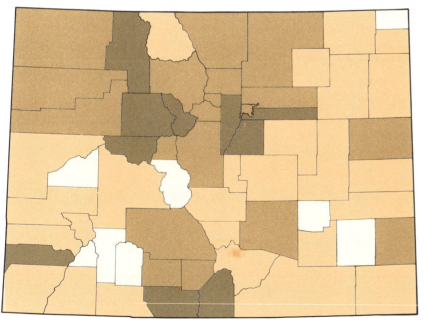

 Over +1.0 Poverty very large compared to county income

 0.0 to +1.0 Poverty moderately large compared to county income

0.0 to -1.0 Poverty moderately small compared to county income

 Below -1.0 Poverty very small compared to county income

INCOME DISTRIBUTION
1980

Source: U.S. Census of Population and Housing, 1980

Land Use

A MAP OF GENERALIZED land use provides a suitable focus for this atlas. Some terms—such as sodbusters, mountain men, and cliff dwellers—have appeared in earlier sections, and suggest historic uses of the land associated with specific groups of people. Other terms define the nature of Colorado geography: the three-fold division into plains, mountains, and plateaus. Modern land uses also reinforce these divisions. Taking some liberty, farming implies the plains; recreation, forestry, and watershed uses relate to the mountains; and grazing, farming, and woodland uses characterize the plateaus. A smattering of urban uses, particularly along the mountain–plains line, fills out the broad associations of land and use.

Urbanized Areas. Cities over 10,000 population (1980) and their contiguous built-up areas are considered urbanized in this simplified system of land use. Residential sectors dominate the urbanized area compared to industrial and business zones. Increasingly larger parts of the city are now given to transportation uses: railroad yards, airport complexes, freeways and city streets, and parking facilities. Hidden by this narrow definition are the many small towns, industrial parks, subdivisions, and other urban uses in the Front Range corridor that lack contiguity with an urban place.

Agriculture. Cultivation of the soil distinguishes agricultural land from grazing land. Cultivated areas may be broken down further into irrigated land (including orchards) and dry farmlands. For mapping purposes mottled patterns of cropland, forest, and range were grouped in a third category, cropland, mixed grazing, and forest.

Irrigation agriculture in eastern Colorado is concentrated in three distinct areas: 1.) the lower Platte with a corn-hogs-cattle emphasis; 2.) the northern piedmont with corn-sugar beets-vegetables-livestock combina-tions; and 3.) the lower Arkansas with melons-sorghum-alfalfa-hogs. A fourth, but rather indistinct area, often mixed with grazing and based on groundwater irrigation of corn, occupies the eastern borderlands. In western Colorado the San Luis Valley with its emphasis on potatoes and barley constitutes the largest irrigated tract. The western plateau country is particularly suited to irrigation. Dams across sharply defined canyons trap winter runoff and feed water to hot, low-lying valleys where the combination of heat, water, and alluvial soil provides ideal growing conditions. Prominent irrigated areas include the Gunnison-Uncompahgre lowlands (Montrose-Delta) and the Grand Valley (Grand Junction-Fruita) where orchards, melons, and vegetables are specialties. Numerous narrow, small, irrigated lowlands are given almost wholly to hay crops, most especially the scattered tracts in the three mountain parks.

Dry farming on the eastern plains means strip cultivation of winter wheat and in the southeast wheat and milo (sorghum) combinations. On the Western Slope, the Dove Creek dry farming area produces a pinto bean specialty.

Grazing. The dominant land use in the state is grazing. Virtually all of the uncultivated portions of the eastern plains, excluding urban use, are devoted to grazing on short grass and scrub ranges. The plateau country of western Colorado supports cattle and sheep herds on the sagebrush and scrub woodlands (juniper and oak). Summer range within national forests, usually lower and peripheral, is secured by lease arrangements with district rangers who evaluate range capacities in animal unit months (AUMs) and limit herd size, time, and distribution according to individual range characteristics.

Forest Lands. Except for some state forests and a few small private holdings, the U.S. government owns and manages the state's forest lands that correspond to mountain lands. Under the Forest Service and Bureau of Land Management, these forests are managed under the concept of multiple use for the maintenance of watersheds, production of wood, grazing, recreation, and wildlife (Multiple Use–Sustained Yield Act of 1960). In Colorado wood production receives lesser emphasis; water retention and storage, camping, wilderness, fishing, hunting, forage, and wildlife habitat receive more. Colorado's mining past with its dense network of old wagon roads and railroad grades makes much of the forest land highly accessible.

Alpine Areas. The elevated timberline ecotone, the tundra and rocky peaks, comprise perhaps the most picturesque scenery in the state. Land use options are extremely limited: watershed, highland wildlife refuge, and some mining. Of active human uses, the prominent activity is recreation, particularly skiing in the timberline ecotone.

A review of topical maps such as landforms, soils, vegetation, climate, farm products, population distribution, economic types, transportation, and environmental quality provides striking comparisons with the land use map and suggests the subtle relationships between land use, natural conditions, and human choice that have created Colorado's tripartite geography.

SELECTED REFERENCES

Colorado Land Use Commission. Map of Existing Land Use, 1:500,000 (1973).

U.S. Geological Survey. Land Use and Land Cover Maps, Colorado, 1:250,000 (1979–83).

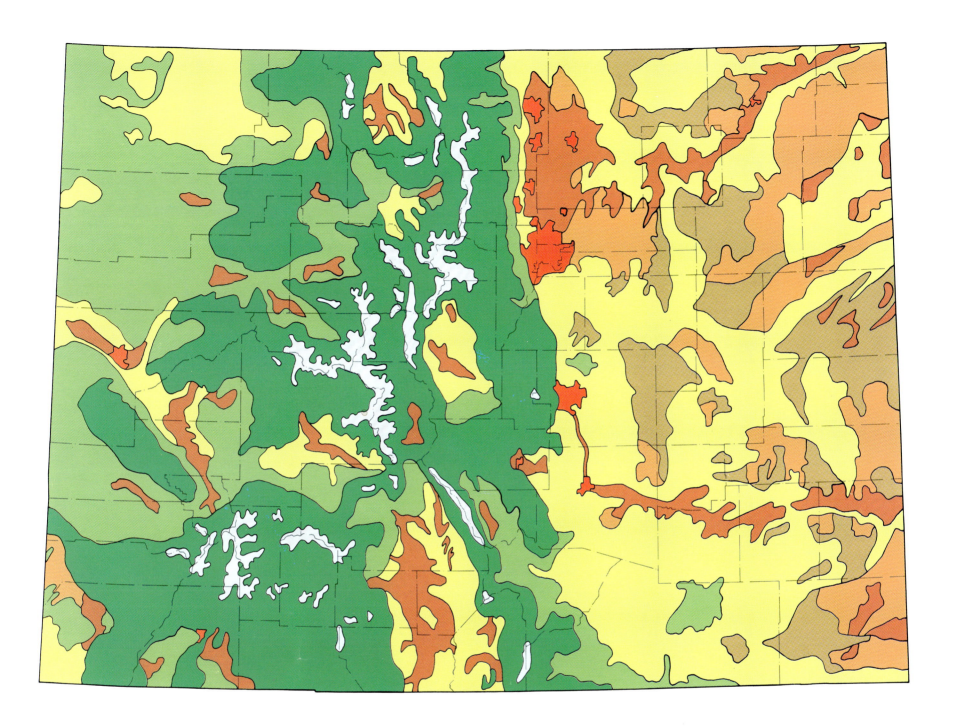

Use Classification

LAND USE

Sources: State Land Use Commission, U.S. Geological Survey

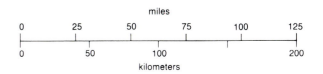

47

A Changing Section

AT ONE TIME, change was something appreciated only by "oldtimers." Today, as the pace of change has quickened, all generations are conscious of the ephemeral nature of known landscapes.

Few changes have been so sweeping or dramatic as those that have occurred in the once-open range and farmlands near Denver's growing periphery. To illustrate the scale and rapidity of change in the Front Range landscape, an entire section (a mile on a side) was chosen in Aurora, an Arapahoe County suburb in the southeastern metropolitan area. With equal effect, the choice could have been a square mile in the Denver contact zone with Jefferson, Boulder, or Adams Counties. For that matter, a similar changing section could be found east of Colorado Springs, west of Longmont or Loveland, or south of Fort Collins.

Essentially, the section of land on this and the facing page is really a microcosm of the ever-sprawling residential landscape of the Front Range corridor. Between 1970 and 1980 the Denver–Boulder metropolitan area gained 375,897 people — in other words, a sizeable city of nearly 400,000 had to be created in the Denver area in just ten years. Fort Collins, the fourth fastest growing metropolitan area in the nation, jumped from 89,900 to 149,278 population, a change of 66%, in only 10 years. Colorado Springs increased by nearly 80,000 (1980 SMSA pop.: 317,584) in the same decade. The tangible product of such staggering growth is, of course, the visible process called urbanization. In just 10 years the farm landscape of the sample section has become "urbanized."

1972. The only residence on the entire square mile is the Summer Valley Ranch, a cluster of cottonwoods with an arcuate shelterbelt on the north side. A small intermittent stream, West Toll Gate Creek, flows from south to north. Except for the ranch, the section is treeless and given over to wheat cultivation and grazing. A dirt road connects the ranch to gravelled, section-line county roads on the north and south sides.

1978 (June). The change has been sudden. Two-lane, asphalt roads now bound the section on the west and north boundaries. Although the ranch itself remains intact, construction activity dominates the farm landscape. Residential units have penetrated along new curvilinear streets and cul-de-sacs in the west and east areas of the section. Where new units are not under actual construction, new streets have been laid out and future cluster sites graded.

1982 (August). The transformation is nearly complete. The remaining undeveloped areas comprise only about 25% of the section, and they are in the process of being developed. The new Cimmaron elementary school overshadows the original ranch along the disappearing creek bed. On the eastern edge the grounds of a new middle school, Horizon, provide some open space. In the southwest corner of the section the Summer Valley Shopping Center has opened; four-lane streets etch the section boundaries on the west, north, and east. The accompanying aerial photograph depicts the final outcome. The reorganization of the entire section has taken less than 10 years to complete and in doing so has erased virtually all the vestiges of an earlier way of life.

1972

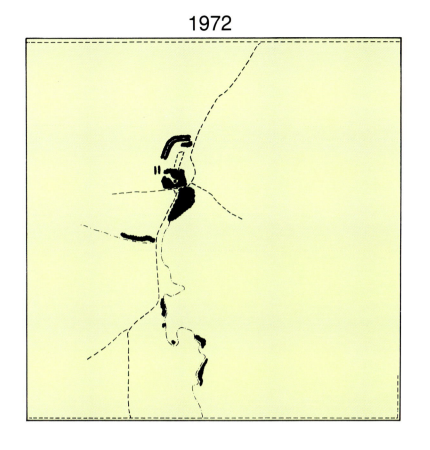

1978

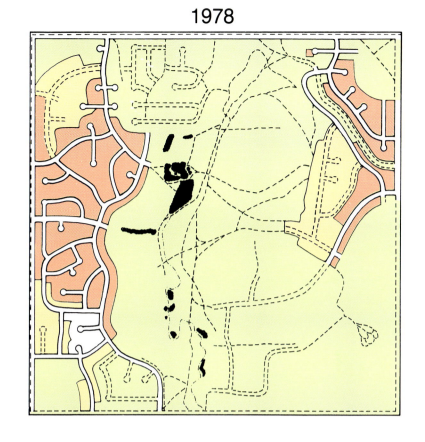

1982

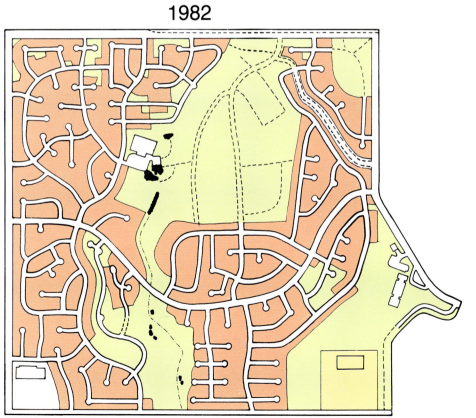

SECTION LOCATION

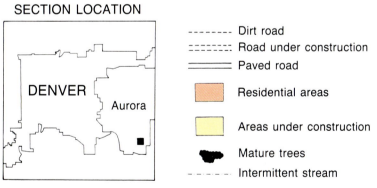

DENVER

Aurora

--------- Dirt road

-------- Road under construction

========= Paved road

Residential areas

Areas under construction

Mature trees

—·—·— Intermittent stream

A CHANGING SECTION

1972 to 1982

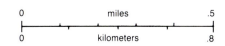

	miles	
0		.5
0	kilometers	.8

Denver's Business District, 1880 to 1890

THE DOWNTOWN OF a city is the focal point of commercial activity. It is the CBD, planning jargon for the Central Business District, characterized by retail stores and shops, business offices and institutions, a high volume of pedestrian traffic, and today, by high-rise buildings. The CBD's definition hinges on precise measurement of the intensity of use by retail stores and offices over contiguous blocks. Historic CBD definitions, such as those on the right, pose increasingly greater difficulties working back into time. Thus, the delineation used on the maps relies on non-quantitative material, such as a listing of business types by address as they appear in *Polk's Directory*, a standard business reference that goes back over 100 years. The precise square-footage measurements are lost, but a reasonably good demarcation of CBD functions occurs and half-block contiguity can be plotted.

Over the last century Denver's downtown area has shifted southeastward and has changed from a space-consumptive horizontal CBD to a vertical CBD. In the backwash of such historic moves, a zone of discarded business structures follows; on the leading edge, the construction of the most modern structures advances. These two underlying historic themes (spatial shift and increasing verticality) relate to architectural advances that quickly outmoded buildings of an earlier CBD. Breakthroughs in water pumping, forced-air heating, and elevator transport

BUSINESS

Parking   Parking

Residence   Residence

were necessary precursors of the spectacular transformation of the CBD by ever taller buildings with ever greater total footage. The transformation has allowed the development of an areally more compact business district while at the same time accommodating a larger clientele. The taller, more densely populated CBD has also brought into being the nocturnally deserted encircling ring of parking lots and garages, a striking contrast to the immediate wall of high-rise business buildings.

The Early Site. The accompanying bird's-eye view of the 1859 site depicts Denver's earliest CBD, a store on the left bank (Auraria) of Cherry Creek. The string of log structures on the Denver side of the creek probably lie along what was shortly to become Larimer Street, named for General Larimer who in turn named the left bank settlement for the Kansas Governor, James Denver. The wooden business district along Larimer burned in 1863 and was quickly rebuilt in brick to become the business strip of Denver for the next two to three decades. By 1880 Denver had grown into a raucous frontier city of 35,000 people.

1880–1900. During the two decades before 1900, Denver emerged as the regional center of the High Plains and adjoining Rocky Mountain mining industry. Population surpassed 100,000 by the turn of the century. Although Larimer retained its commercial vigor, the CBD began sprawling up 16th Street with "high-rise" buildings of five stories, epitomized by the famed Brown Palace Hotel. The completion of the Capitol further reinforced the southeastward trend and, by 1900, the CBD reached its maximum area size covering the length of Larimer from Broadway to 14th Street and two to three blocks on each side of 16th Street.

1920–1940. The parallel 15th-16th-17th strip of blocks from Larimer to Glenarm became Denver's CBD during the interwar years. Larimer Street, only comprising a few blocks of the CBD in 1920, became by 1940 a discarded business area soon to be characterized

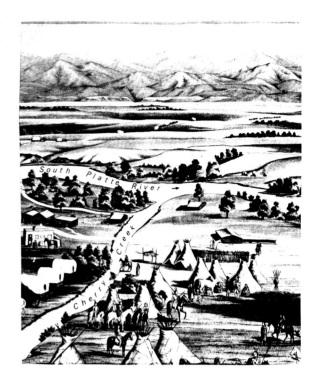

by pawn shops, saloons, flophouses, and a skid row population.

1960–1980. The southeastward migration of the CBD seems to have played out during these twenty years: in 1960 the southern boundary had crossed Broadway–16th abutting the public land of Capitol Hill and City Hall; by 1980 the CBD had withdrawn to the northeast of 16th on paralleling 17th and 18th, leaving a new zone of discard on 14th-15th. Many of Larimer's shabby but picturesque nineteenth century brick and stone buildings were razed and replaced with parking lots. The resulting compactness of the 1980 delineation affords a noteworthy contrast with earlier CBDs.

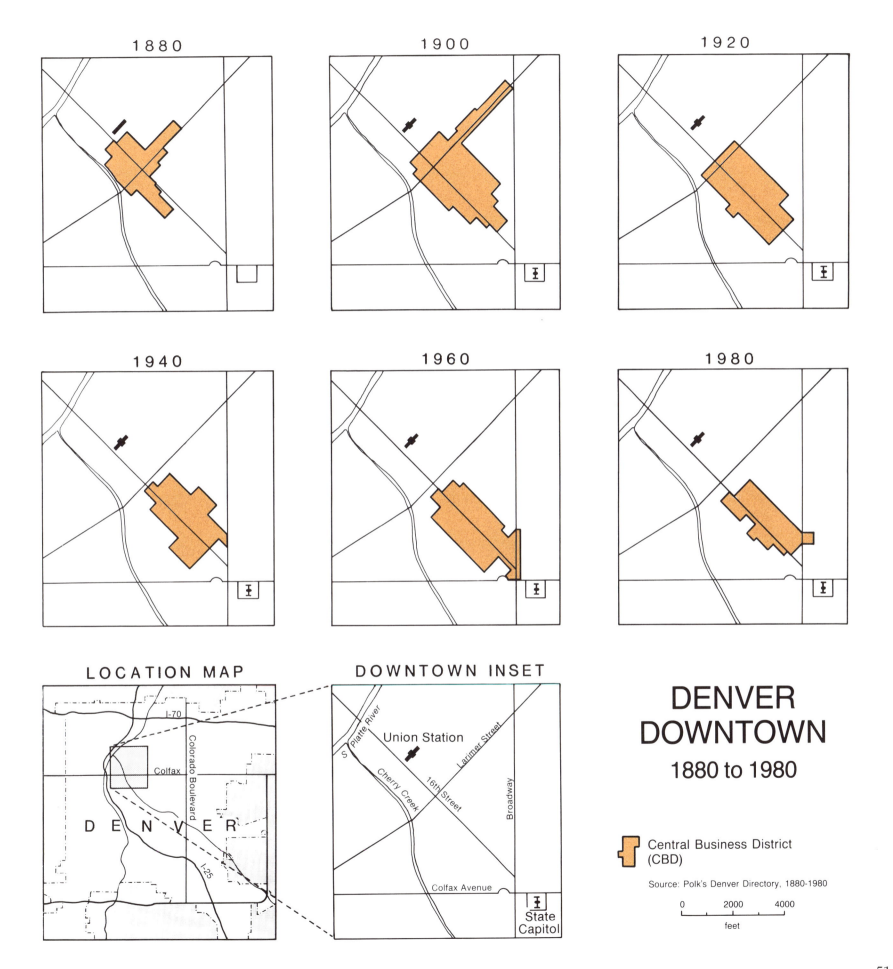

1880

1900

1920

1940

1960

1980

LOCATION MAP

I-70

Colfax

Colorado Boulevard

D E N V E R

I-25

DOWNTOWN INSET

S Platte River

Union Station

Cherry Creek

16th Street

Larimer Street

Broadway

Colfax Avenue

State Capitol

DENVER DOWNTOWN

1880 to 1980

Central Business District (CBD)

Source: Polk's Denver Directory, 1880-1980

0   2000   4000

feet

Economic Production

ECONOMIC PRODUCTION comprises those things of value that are produced, exchanged, and consumed. For cartographers, these activities can possess a spatial dimension. The map on the facing page emphasizes production based on the percentage of the employed population in each county that is engaged in one of three production types: 1.) *primary*, which includes the direct extraction and use of natural resources, traditionally mining, forestry, fishing, and agriculture; 2.) *secondary*, which encompasses the activities that add value to products through processing (for food or fiber), refining (petroleum), or fabrication (metals); and 3.) *tertiary*, which comprises the service industries, or those activities that do not directly produce anything but rather serve the population.[1] Put another way, these three production types are often referred to as *extractive*, *industrial*, and *service*, terms hereafter used.

Two kinds of distribution emerge from a comparison of these activities in the state. One distribution is graphical, plotted conveniently on a triangular graph and showing each county as a dot placed according to employment percentages in that county. The resulting economic emphases allow the development of economic types based on employment orientation. The county types produce a second, areal distribution across the state as shown on the facing page.

Extractive Economies. Seventeen of Colorado's 63 counties have over 25% of the employed population engaged in extractive occupations, essentially mining and farming. An old rule of thumb allows that one industrial or extractive worker will support about three service people. Worker populations that comprise over 25% of the labor force will

exceed the 1:3 ratio and indicate a proportionately low service role in the local economy. The accompanying triangular graph relies on the 25% line as a threshold for extractive definition (as it also does for industrial definition).

The sparsely populated High Plains counties that are located away from the service centers along the Platte and Arkansas valleys typically show farm workers making up 30–35% of the employed population, giving the counties a strong rural and small town flavor. Distances to a variety of supporting services are great, often to another county. Services in the county seat will depend directly on the status of agriculture and, rather naturally, conversation will revolve around crops, farm prices, and the latest machinery and agricultural techniques.

A prime (') symbol designates an extreme emphasis on extractive economy and pertains to eight counties where over 35% of the labor force depends on extraction. On the upper end of this dependence are three small mountain counties, Lake, Mineral, and San Juan, where a strong emphasis on mining is reinforced by some ranching and forestry to give extractive levels around the 45% level. The other extremes include the "wide open spaces" of ranching and farming found on the High Plains (Kiowa, Cheyenne, and Washington counties), in North Park (Jackson), and on isolated mountain and plateau country (Dolores).

Industrial Economies. Among the 50 states, Colorado is hardly noteworthy for its industrial contribution, although it has regional importance (see later section on manufacturing). Industrial workers, even including construction, exceed 25% of the labor force in only 6 of the state's 63 counties and none of these counties qualify for industrial designation.

The leading industrial counties reflect the recent trend in the Front Range corridor toward dispersal and growth of light industry (particularly "high tech" industries) and toward sprawling residential growth which includes the construction worker component. Larimer County, which many Coloradans

might associate with mountains, ranches, and good fishing, leads all counties in industrial emphasis, due in part to the establishment of extensive Hewlett-Packard operations there. Boulder, Adams, and Douglas are close behind as industrial counties. Park County, essentially the high basin called South Park, stands as an exception to the Front Range corridor pattern. A high number of construction workers in 1980 and a small population base would indicate that Park County's industrial status will be short-lived. Pueblo, right on the 25% line, owes its character to a long-standing heavy industrial base of iron and steel production.

Service Economies. The service-oriented counties, 8 in all, may be differentiated into two sub-types: 1.) regional centers that centralize major services such as banking, radio and newspapers, and retail and wholesale trade. At one scale is Denver; at lesser scales are Durango and Alamosa. 2.) Resort counties, catering especially to skiers where food services, building maintenance, transportation, and entertainment-recreational service comprise an important segment in the economy. In Pitkin County (Aspen) the service sector accounts for 82% of employment, a percentage higher than Denver's.

Diversified Economies. Thirty-two counties, just over half of all counties, fall into a classification that displays a balance between industrial (17%), extractive (17%), and service sectors (66%). These counties also include many regionally important service centers such as Grand Junction, Montrose, Craig, Rifle, Fort Morgan, Sterling, and La Junta.

---

[1]From the 1980 Census, construction and manufacturing were combined for secondary employment; transportation, communications and public utilities, wholesale and retail trade, finance, insurance, and real estate, business and repair service, and personal, entertainment, and recreational services are combined for commercial service.

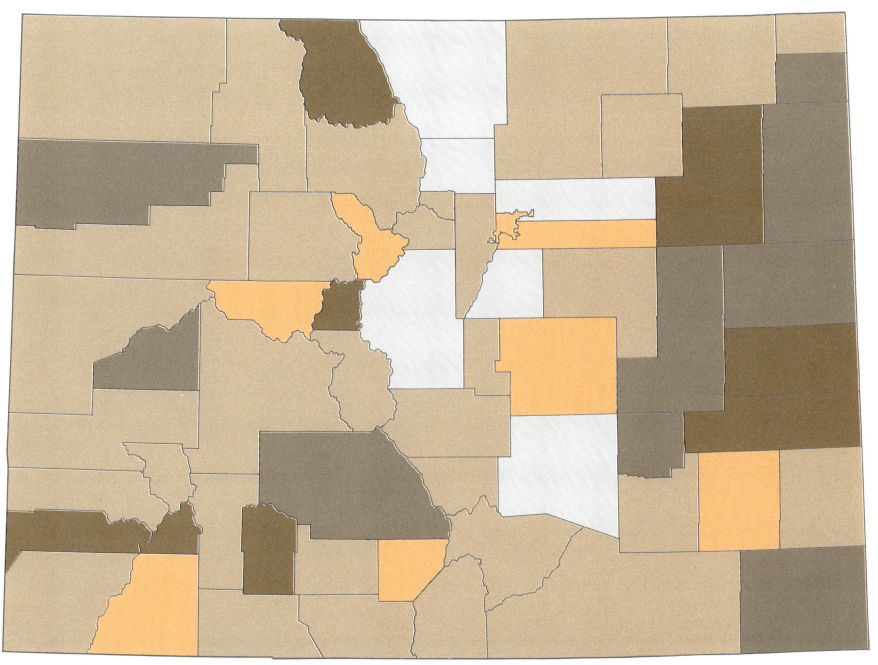

County Economic Emphasis

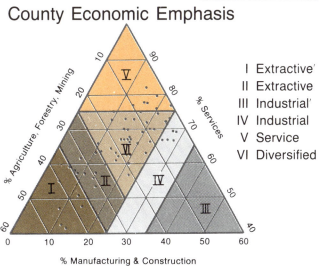

I Extractive
II Extractive
III Industrial
IV Industrial
V Service
VI Diversified

% Agriculture, Forestry, Mining

% Services

% Manufacturing & Construction

COUNTY ECONOMY
Employment Distribution

Source: U.S. Census of Population, 1980

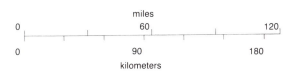

miles
0   60   120

0   90   180
kilometers

Agriculture

FARM PRODUCTS. The last published Census of Agriculture (1978) indicated that sales of agricultural products amounted to $2.6 billion, making the farm economy second among economic activities in the state; only manufacturing generated more dollars. Further, many industrial products are derived directly from conversion (e.g., distilling, refining, milling) of farm output. Indirectly, services (such as transportation) that contribute to the state's economy may show a strong agricultural component. In short, farm sales alone constitute a less than adequate measure of the role of agricultural production in the total economy of the state.

A traditional breakdown of farm products would segregate crops, livestock, and poultry; and in Colorado these product categories account for $574 million, $1,971 million, and $60 million, respectively, in sales (1978). Clearly, livestock and livestock products (milk, cheese, wool, etc.) dominate the state's agriculture, making up 75% of total farm sales, but hidden in this dominance of livestock are unsold crops, especially corn for silage and alfalfa, grown to feed livestock.

Crops. The traditional crop of the Great Plains is wheat, dryfarmed across the great stretches from the Texas panhandle to North Dakota. Indeed, initial "sod-busting" on the Plains in the late nineteenth and early twentieth centuries is, in the minds of many, so closely associated with wheat farming that an image remains of unbroken wheat fields stretching beyond the Mississippi River. This image, however, highly distorts the true picture of agriculture on the plains and of diversified farming in Colorado.

To be sure, wheat retains some historical importance with the easternmost Colorado counties displaying a concentration of wheat production connected to the Kansas core of the winter wheat belt. A sizeable production of wheat also persists across Adams and Arapahoe Counties east of Denver and on the uplands north of the Platte Valley to the Wyoming border.

But as measured by volume (bushels) of grain products, Colorado's premier crop is corn. Nearly 80 million bushels were produced in 1978 — nearly 20 million more than wheat. Additionally, corn for silage and green chop made up another 4.6 million tons of production. As an irrigated crop in Colorado, the distribution of corn farming includes three sharply delineated concentrations: 1.) the well-watered piedmont north of Denver; 2.) the narrow Platte Valley northeastward to Nebraska; and 3.) sprinkler irrigation based on groundwater in the Ogallala formation on the northeastern border, particularly in Yuma County which now produces nearly one-third of the state's corn crop.

Barley, oats, and sorghums account for the remainder of the grains grown in the state. All three are feed grains closely associated with the livestock industry; barley, when malted for brewing, constitutes an industrial crop. Barley and oats share a similar distribution although 12 times as much barley is produced in the state. The most notable concentration of both grains occurs in the San Luis Valley. The sorghums, particularly drought-tolerant milo, are almost exclusively an aspect of southern plains agriculture in the Arkansas Valley and Baca County in the southeast corner of the state. Alfalfa, a closely allied component of the feed grains, appears on irrigated stretches of most river valleys in the state, notably the Arkansas, Platte, Rio Grande (San Luis Valley), Gunnison, with traces along the upper Colorado and Yampa rivers. Again, the irrigated piedmont with its concentration on livestock production appears as a notable area of alfalfa cultivation.

Specialty crops in Colorado reveal distinct distribution patterns. Nearly one-half of all potatoes grown in the state are grown in a single county, Rio Grande, in the San Luis Valley. By weight, 85% of all potatoes grown in Colorado come from the five counties of the San Luis Valley, an area that began as a specialty in Red McClure potatoes in 1913. Sugar beet cultivation, an industrial crop dating from the early 1900s, is a distinct specialty of the piedmont and the Platte Valley. Vegetables and melons by acreage in production illustrate the marked clustering of specialty crops: the piedmont, the middle Arkansas (particularly melons), and to a lesser degree the San Luis Valley and the Uncompahgre around Montrose. Dry field beans and seed beans appear throughout the irrigated croplands of northeastern Colorado, but the highest concentration of production (pinto beans) occurs in the southwestern corner of the state centered around Dove Creek. The pattern of bean specialties is completed with mention of the lower Gunnison and the distinct area of northeastern El Paso County. Orchard crops show a pattern as exclusive as that of potatoes. Nearly 84% of the state's entire acreage of tree crops can be found along the Uncompahgre and Colorado rivers in Delta and Mesa counties where apples offer further specialization.

Livestock. A dot map of livestock distribution is less reliable than crop distributions for a number of reasons: mobility, production variability, season of census, and different feeding patterns. The accompanying maps therefore represent approximate locations for the census year 1978.

All but the most rugged mountain counties show at least 5,000 head of cattle, which gives a rather even pattern of cattle numbers across the entire state with notable feedlot concentration in the piedmont and Platte Valley. Sheep, more clearly range animals, are associated with the plateau and valley country of western Colorado — with the exception of the Weld County concentration on the northern piedmont. In western Colorado the sheep population shows a slightly higher density in the San Luis Valley and adjoining range and in the northwestern corner of the state. Hogs and pigs, dependent on feed grain production, are predictably localized in the irrigated valleys and piedmont.

Farm Characteristics. A look at the detailed characteristics of farming in Colorado reveals a wide variation among the counties. These

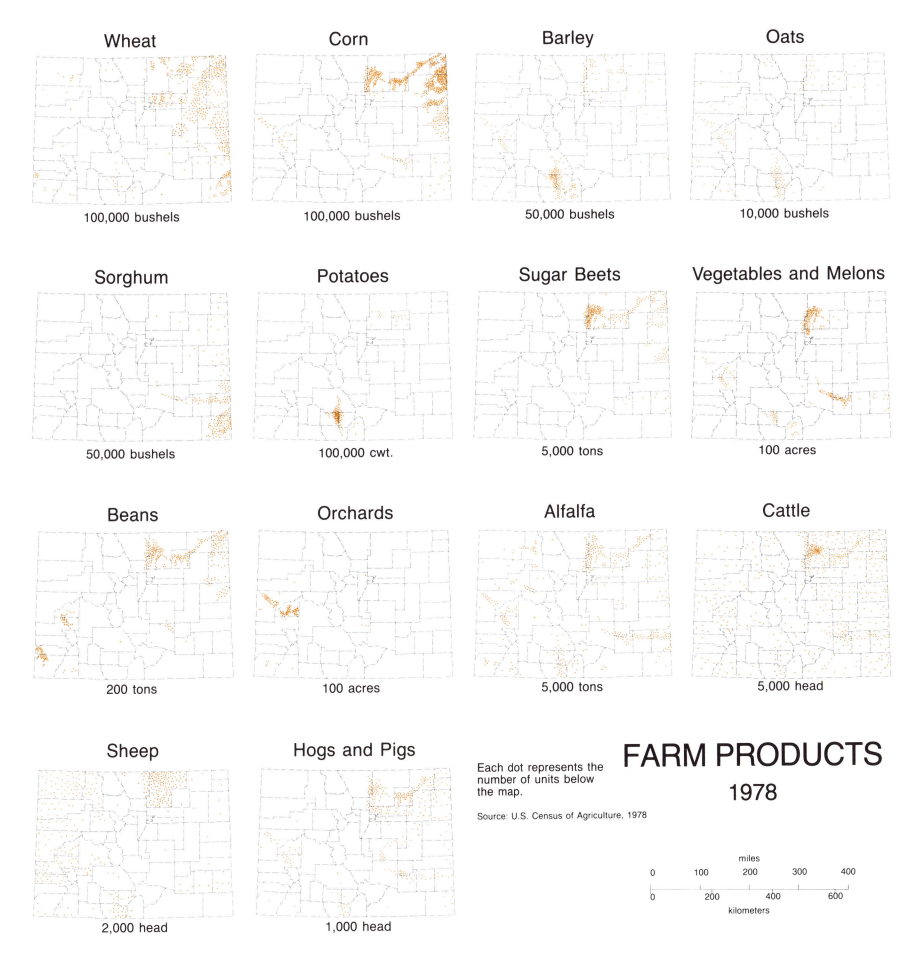

Wheat
100,000 bushels

Corn
100,000 bushels

Barley
50,000 bushels

Oats
10,000 bushels

Sorghum
50,000 bushels

Potatoes
100,000 cwt.

Sugar Beets
5,000 tons

Vegetables and Melons
100 acres

Beans
200 tons

Orchards
100 acres

Alfalfa
5,000 tons

Cattle
5,000 head

Sheep
2,000 head

Hogs and Pigs
1,000 head

Each dot represents the number of units below the map.

Source: U.S. Census of Agriculture, 1978

FARM PRODUCTS
1978

miles
0   100   200   300   400

0   200   400   600
kilometers

differences in turn reflect the variety of physical, economic, and cultural conditions encountered in the state. Overall, the accompanying maps illustrate that farming tends to conform to the persistent, differentiating theme of plains, mountains, and plateaus in Colorado's geography.

Cropland

The size of a county quite naturally determines the amount of cropland it will have. Therefore, all things being equal, it is reasonable to expect the larger counties to show the greater cropland acreages and, in the case of Weld and Washington, the expectation holds. These two counties contain 1,745,311 acres of cropland, 16% of the state's land in crops. Land quality provides the other governing factor in cropland distribution and clearly sets off the plains from the mountains and plateaus, where climate and terrain severely restrict arable lands to limited lowlands and parks.

Irrigation Dependence

The dependence of farming on irrigation is expressed here as the ratio of irrigated land to cropland. The resulting percentages may be somewhat inflated from the inclusion of irrigated pasture (non-cropland) in the figures, particularly on the Western Slope. Generally, the map suggests a reversal of the cropland distribution. No fewer than 12 counties, all with little available cropland, rely almost totally (over 95%) on irrigation. The counties below the statewide average of 35% have a notable plains concentration where dryfarming dominates. However, there are exceptions: 1.) the middle Arkansas Valley with Otero and Bent counties where irrigated land accounts for over 60% of the cropland; 2.) the northern piedmont where farming depends on water impoundment and irrigation; 3.) the Morgan and Logan county irrigated strip along the South Platte; and 4.) Yuma County with groundwater-based irrigation.

Farm Output

The average value of farm products per farm indicates the most productive (in dollars) farms in the state. The figure would indicate to a lesser degree the location of the wealthier farms although production costs, such as machinery or land rent, will alter individual farm incomes. One county alone, Weld County, contributes 31% of the state's total agricultural production. Each of Weld's 3,178 farms produced an average of $258,091 in the year of the last census (1978). Crowley showed a higher average of $282,889 per farm, but included only 249 farms for the county.

Farm Machinery Investment

The strip of 6 counties along the eastern border illustrates the high machinery investment, over $57,000 per farm, that is associated with the plowing, planting, fertilizing, protecting, and harvesting of grains, in this case corn and wheat. Highly mechanized agriculture also shows up with potatoes and barley in Rio Grande County. Generally, where the irrigation dependence is low, the machinery dependence is high.

Farm Size

An interesting comparison exists between average farm size and average farm output (upper right). The three most productive counties have farm sizes below the county mean of 1,600 acres, pointing to the intensity of agriculture in Weld, Morgan, and Crowley counties. The farms of four rangeland counties (Moffat, Jackson, Park, and Las Animas) average over 3,700 acres per farm or ranch, yet rank low in individual farm production. The old family cattle and sheep ranches are often maintained not so much for income than to preserve a vanishing way of life.

Tenure

Statewide, only 54% of farmers own all the land on which they operate. All or a large part of farmland may be leased for extensive grain production where investment in machinery may override investment in the land itself. This relationship appears clearly in the eastern wheat counties where the percentage of full owners falls below 41. Typically, the part-owner has increased the acreage in order to meet ever-mounting costs of production. The expansion can occur where there is land available for lease, such as may be created by death within an old farm family with offspring unwilling to operate the farmstead, or where there is sufficient credit available to buy adjoining farmland. Rather characteristically, full ownership is higher where production cycles have a long duration, such as in orchards, and the Colorado–Gunnison triangle of counties shows well on this characteristic.

Absentee Farmers

With increasing mobility and mechanization, many farmers have abandoned the isolated farmstead, choosing rather the amenities of small town life. The modern "sidewalk farmer" commutes to the farm or to scattered parcels (if leased) and completes relatively quickly, thanks to power machinery, the traditional tasks of cultivation, planting, and harvesting. For about one out of five farmers in the wheat counties of the eastern plains this is a way of life. Notable areas of nonresident farming also occur among the pinto bean farmers of Dolores County and among the ranchers and alfalfa growers of Moffat County.

Age of Farmers

The pattern of older farmers corresponds well to the counties where ranching remains an important agricultural enterprise. The age of farmers here reinforces the role of tradition in ranching as opposed to purely economic forms of livelihood. Younger farmers typify the more highly mechanized, productive, part-owner farms of the plains.

Sample Farms. The maps on page 59 depict three sample farms selected as representative of typical agricultural land use in Colorado. The maps are based on discussions with the county agents and farm operators, and are drawn from pertinent aerial photographs. All three farms are located in Weld County, an area that epitomizes the wealth and diversity of Colorado agricultural production.

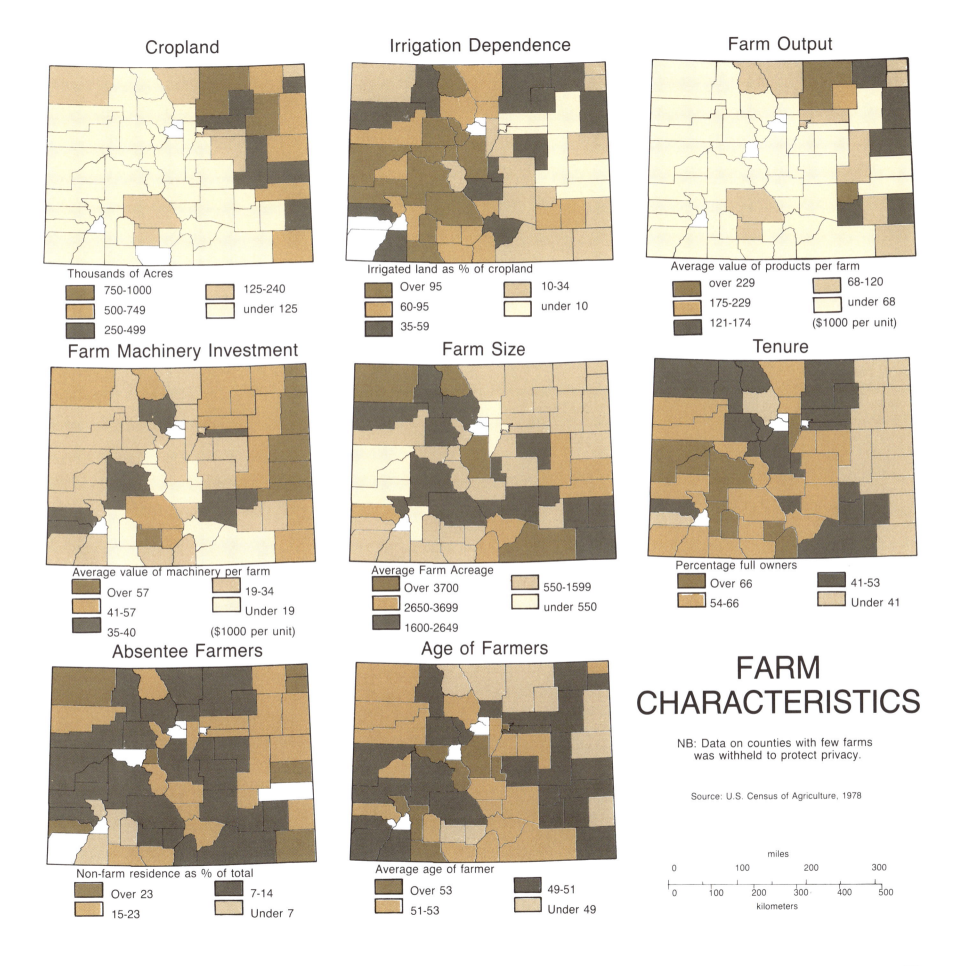

Cropland

Thousands of Acres
- 750-1000
- 500-749
- 250-499
- 125-240
- under 125

Irrigation Dependence

Irrigated land as % of cropland
- Over 95
- 60-95
- 35-59
- 10-34
- under 10

Farm Output

Average value of products per farm
- over 229
- 175-229
- 121-174
- 68-120
- under 68
($1000 per unit)

Farm Machinery Investment

Average value of machinery per farm
- Over 57
- 41-57
- 35-40
- 19-34
- Under 19
($1000 per unit)

Farm Size

Average Farm Acreage
- Over 3700
- 2650-3699
- 1600-2649
- 550-1599
- under 550

Tenure

Percentage full owners
- Over 66
- 54-66
- 41-53
- Under 41

Absentee Farmers

Non-farm residence as % of total
- Over 23
- 15-23
- 7-14
- Under 7

Age of Farmers

Average age of farmer
- Over 53
- 51-53
- 49-51
- Under 49

FARM CHARACTERISTICS

NB: Data on counties with few farms was withheld to protect privacy.

Source: U.S. Census of Agriculture, 1978

miles
0   100   200   300

0   100   200   300   400   500
kilometers

Irrigated Farm

Only a 238-acre parcel of a 1,500-acre farm is shown. This farm comprises 11 separate pieces of land that are scattered across 18 miles. Although the dispersed holdings resulted from haphazard acquisition, the distances between land parcels reduce the chance of complete crop loss by minimizing the amount of land exposed to localized weather phenomena such as hail or wind storms.

The operator rotates 3 crops on a 3-year cycle, although only one of the crops, onions, is the principal cash crop. Rotation of other crops with onions is necessary to prevent the build-up of host-specific diseases in the soil and to restore vital nutrients and organic matter to the soil. A leguminous crop in the cycle, beans in this case, provides for periodic replenishment of nitrogen without resorting to heavy applications of artificial fertilizer. The ideal rotation order of onions, corn for silage, and pinto beans does not apply to all parcels of the farm because some of the land is rented. Crops such as silage corn do not return enough to pay rent on the land and thus tenure arrangements in this sample directly affect incentives to monocrop. In addition, a small amount of alfalfa is grown, but not regularly rotated with other crops.

The onion yield on this farm falls within the average range of 350–450 hundred-pound bags per acre. Onions, harvested by hand, are a labor-intensive crop: the farm employs only 7 full-time people, but hires an additional 100 for the harvest in late August to early October.

Concrete troughs carry water from a large county ditch to the fields which, gently inclined, allow the water to run from the troughs through 8-inch-deep furrows across the full extent of the fields.

Wheat Ranch

The map of the dryland wheat farm to the right shows 1,000 acres of a 4,800-acre unit. Since 1935 the same family has owned the farmland over which hard winter wheat (bread wheat) alternates with strips of summer fallow. Wheat is planted on alternate strips of land in late August and September and is harvested in mid-July. After the harvest the strips are left as summer fallow for a year with a stubble mulch cover. The mulch cover helps conserve moisture, prevents erosion, and adds essential nutrients to the soil. The rested strips are planted about 13 months after their last harvesting. Although in a given year only half of the land is under production, strip farming turns out to be cost-effective over the long run as soil depletion slows, yields stabilize, and wind and water erosion diminishes.

Grain yields under strip farming in this area can range up to 60 bushels per acre, although 30–35 bushels is a more realistic figure, and in the case of extreme drought or locally intense weather, may be zero bushels per acre. The farmer on this sample unit aims for a minimum of 30 bushels per acre, but occasionally yield will dip below this target. Three people work year-round on the farm and 3 or 4 extra hands are hired on during the summer to help with the harvest and planting.

The operator also maintains about 30 head of stock cattle as an additional source of income. Cattle graze on the 3 sections of rangeland shown on the map. This range has enough surface water so that the farmer finds it unnecessary to pump well water. Calves are sold at market price when they reach 500–600 pounds.

Union Pacific owns the oil and natural gas rights of odd-numbered sections on the farm. The railway, in turn, leases these rights to oil companies. Two and a half percent of the profits produced from oil on the farm go back to the owner. The 5 active wells on this property bring in an income of about $5,000 per year.

Cattle Ranch

The third map outlines the entire 3,600 acres of a cattle ranch near Greeley, Colorado. Unlike cattle ranches that raise and fatten large herds of cattle to be sold for beef, this ranch specializes in the sale of registered Hereford bulls that are sold as stud to commercial herds and used to upgrade the quality of the herds.

One hundred head of cattle are cared for on this ranch. Registered Hereford cows are bred in the winter and summer, calving then in the fall and spring, respectively, after a nine-month gestation. From mid-April to January, the cattle graze on different fenced-in parcels of the 3,400 acres of rangeland. Water can be obtained directly from the creek on the property thus obviating the need for wells. The location and condition of the cattle are checked daily by the manager and the owner.

In January, pregnant cows are brought into corrals near the farm buildings to have their calves. Bulls that will be sold are also kept in proximate corrals so that their weight and condition may be closely monitored.

In addition to the owner and his wife, the ranch employs one person full-time and one person part-time. The average income of the ranch is approximately $36,000 per year from the sale of 36–38 bulls. Forty or more cows and heifers are also sold each year. Over and above sales of animals, a small added income ensues from the sale of corn, alfalfa hay, and oats which are grown on the irrigated parcels of land adjacent to the farm buildings and creek. Part of the irrigated land is rented to another farmer who is responsible for the planting and harvesting of the crops. The other irrigated land serves as irrigated pasture and partly as cropland for fodder. Two sections (1,280 acres) of rangeland are leased from the state of Colorado for $1 per acre per year.

SECTION OF IRRIGATED FARM (221 ACRES)

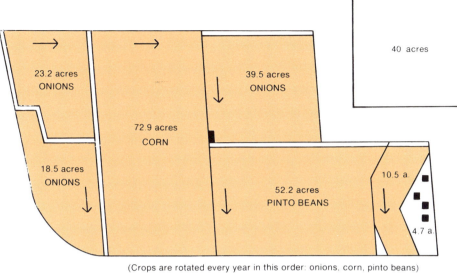

23.2 acres
ONIONS

39.5 acres
ONIONS

72.9 acres
CORN

18.5 acres
ONIONS

52.2 acres
PINTO BEANS

10.5 a.

4.7 a.

40 acres

(Crops are rotated every year in this order: onions, corn, pinto beans)

CATTLE RANCH (3542 ACRES)

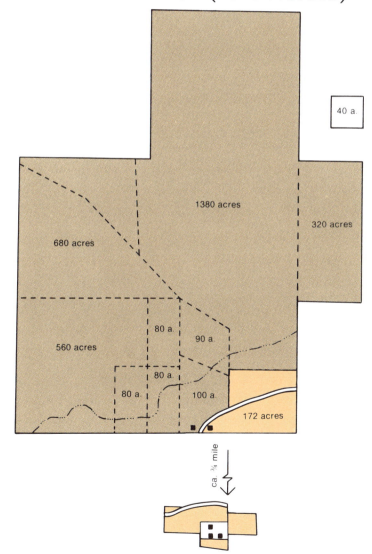

1380 acres

320 acres

680 acres

560 acres

80 a.

90 a.

80 a.

80 a.

100 a.

172 acres

40 a.

ca. ¾ mile

SECTION OF DRYLAND WHEAT FARM (1603 ACRES)

fence line

80 acres

163 acres

40 a.

129 acres

fence line

fence line

THREE FARMS
Weld County

- - - FENCE

-·- CREEK

═══ IRRIGATION TROUGH

→ DIRECTION OF IRRIGATION

■ FARM BUILDING

☐ 40-ACRE SQUARES FOR COMPARISON OF FARM SIZES

RANGE LAND

IRRIGATED LAND

WHEAT

FALLOW

ALTERNATING

Manufacturing

For nearly 100 years after the discovery of gold and the first diversions of water for irrigation, Colorado has been nationally renowned for the products of its mines, farms, and ranches. Historically, miners produced significant quantities of silver, gold, lead, and zinc, but the current emphasis centers on strategic metals and mineral fuels including molybdenum, uranium, oil, gas, and coal. Agriculturally, the state is recognized for the high yields of fruit, feed grains, sugar beets, and potatoes from irrigated oases, for high quality beef from feed lots, and for small grains and sorghums from dryland farms.

These primary activities continue as significant elements in the state's economy; however, during World War II and in the following decade manufacturing expanded so rapidly that by the mid-1950s it became the state's leading industry. This pronounced increase (Graph 1) was spurred by 1.) substantially increased production in long-established "traditional" industries and 2.) the birth and spectacular growth of electronics, space vehicles, and research-oriented facilities. The "traditional" industrial base includes those firms and factories whose raw materials are derived from farms, ranches, and mines, such as grains for milling or brewing, beef for packing, and oil for refining. With some exceptions (Colorado Fuel and Iron at Pueblo and Gates Rubber Company of Denver) this traditional category of manufacturing had a quasi-colonial flavor. Essentially, Colorado processed and exported its local raw materials and imported most of its manufactured goods from the east.

In the postwar era, new clean "high technology" industries that require a highly skilled labor force, research scientists, and a reasonable degree of isolation for testing and security purposes became significant features in the industrial landscape. Typifying this new expansion were the Martin Marietta Company, Denver division, which plays a significant role in the nation's defense and space exploration, and the Beech Aircraft research and development plant in the foothills north of Boulder.

The expansion initiated in the postwar period has continued at an accelerated pace. A few traditional establishments, especially sugar refiners and meat packers, are missing from the industrial scene; however, other manufacturers such as the Adolph Coors Company have repeatedly expanded their markets and facilities. Multi-national organizations, such as Eastman Kodak Company, Hewlett-Packard, and International Business Machine Corporation have established large facilities in the piedmont providing thousands of jobs, whether for Colorado residents or for individuals transferred within the organizations.

These new plants and other "high-tech" facilities were attracted to Colorado for many reasons, including 1.) the availability of talent, ideas, and research data from a large number of universities, colleges, and federal agencies throughout the Front Range corridor; 2.) the opportunity for employees to enjoy an agreeable and salubrious climate characterized by a high percentage of possible sunshine, low relative humidity, and comfortable temperatures; 3.) the informality of western living including easy access to winter and summer recreation areas; 4.) lower costs for land and labor than in the industrial northeast; and 5.) ample space for expansion of plant facilities, for the safe testing of equipment and for a reasonable degree of isolation and security.

Manufacturing is and always has been concentrated along the eastern base of the Rockies, initially in urban settings but now primarily in suburban settings (Table 1).

From 1899 to 1954, more than two-thirds of industrial activity occurred in Denver and Pueblo counties. In the past three decades, however, industrial diversification and decentralization have taken place on a grand scale. Denver County, which accounted for three-fifths of the state's manufacturing until as recently as 1947, now produces less than one-fifth of the industrial output. Manufacturing in Denver actually increased in this period, but its share of the state's total decreased with the accelerated growth along the piedmont. The basic reason for this percentage decline is associated with an unusual geographic fact: the city of Denver and the county of Denver have the same boundaries, providing little room for development. Nearby counties (Boulder, Jefferson, Adams, and Arapahoe) attracted a large share of new industry and they now produce more than two-fifths (43.57%) of the manufacturing total. Four other counties (Larimer, Weld, Pueblo, and El Paso) account for more than one-fourth (25.9%) of the total. This assemblage of 9 counties currently accounts for 94% of the value added by manufacturing, 93% of the employees and 93% of the state's industrial payroll. With only one other county (Mesa) contributing more than 1% of value added, it is readily apparent that manufacturing is relatively insignificant in the 53 counties of the mountains, the plateaus, and the eastern plains.

The industrial corridor along the mountain front from Fort Collins to Pueblo contrasts significantly with the old mill towns of New England or the heavy industrial districts of Chicago-Gary or Pittsburgh-Cleveland. With the exception of the Colorado Fuel and Iron

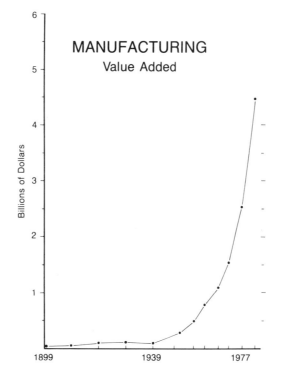

MANUFACTURING
Value Added

Historic Development of Manufacturing

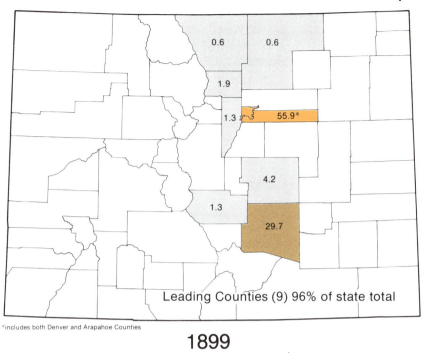

Leading Counties (9) 96% of state total

*includes both Denver and Arapahoe Counties

1899

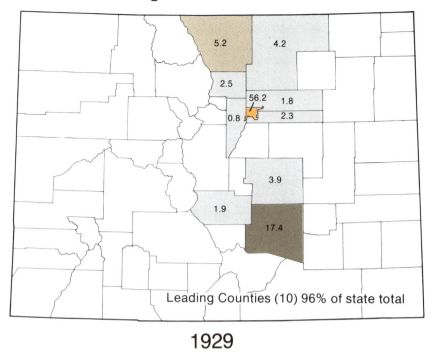

Leading Counties (10) 96% of state total

1929

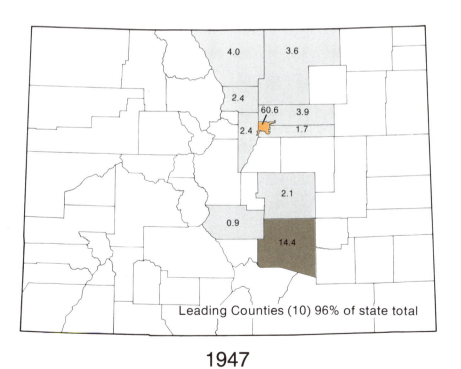

Leading Counties (10) 96% of state total

1947

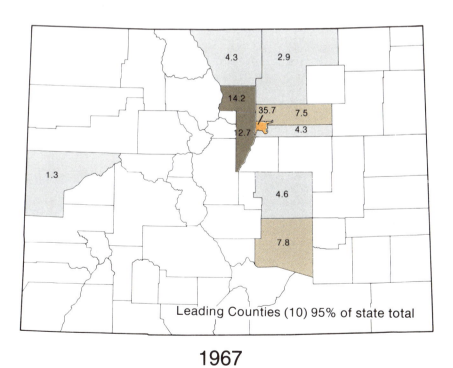

Leading Counties (10) 95% of state total

1967

Table 1. MANUFACTURING – LEADING COUNTIES – 1899-1977
(% of value added)

County	1899	1919	1929	1939	1947	1954	1958	1963	1967	1972	1977
Denver	55.9*	49.8	56.2	57.4	60.6	52.6	45.3	37.2	35.7	31.1	24.8
Jefferson	1.3	0.4	0.8	2.4	2.4	6.0	17.1	28.9	12.7	19.8	15.6
Boulder	1.9	4.4	2.5	1.8	2.4	1.5	1.5	1.7	14.2	9.6	14.1
Adams	–	2.7	1.8	4.1	3.9	7.3	7.2	6.5	7.5	9.2	8.7
Larimer	0.6	6.3	5.2	3.5	4.0	2.2	2.7	3.0	4.3	4.2	7.3
Weld	0.6	3.7	4.2	3.1	3.6	2.2	2.4	2.6	2.9	4.6	6.8
Pueblo	29.7	15.0	17.4	18.5	14.4	16.0	13.1	8.3	7.8	6.4	6.4
El Paso	4.2	2.4	3.9	1.9	2.1	4.0	3.5	2.9	4.6	4.6	5.4
Arapahoe	–	0.5	2.3	1.3	1.7	3.8	3.6	3.3	4.3	3.9	5.1
	94.2	85.2	94.3	94.0	95.1	95.7	96.4	86.1	94.0	93.4	94.2
Mesa	–	–	–	–	–	–	–	0.9	1.3	1.0	1.1
Fremont	1.3	3.7	1.9	1.2	0.9	1.6	1.5	0.8	0.6	0.7	1.0
	95.5	88.9	96.2	95.2	96.0	97.3	97.9	87.8	95.9	95.1	96.3
Others	4.5	11.1	3.8	4.8	4.0	3.7	2.1	12.2	4.1	4.9	3.7

*Includes both Denver and Arapahoe counties.

facility in Pueblo, one of only three fully integrated iron and steel plants in the West, Colorado's industrial landscape is dominated by a combination of long established traditional industries and large numbers of new, clean, light industries frequently situated in semirural settings or in industrial parks on the fringes of major cities. The older industries are typified by food processors, whose products, meat, beverages, and baked goods still head all categories of goods as identified in the Annual Survey of Manufacturing (1978). Machinery, particularly office computing and electronic computing equipment, ranks a strong second and is representative of new establishments. Other significant products in the manufacturing mix are listed in Table 2.

The recent growth and status of manufacturing in Colorado impress most observers of the industrial scene. Since the end of World War II, the growth rate substantially exceeded the national rate in every census period. Regionally, Colorado continues as the industrial leader among the Rocky Mountain states (Table 3), a position it may be expected to retain for reasons suggested earlier. In addition, Denver, the financial center of the Rocky Mountains and energy capital of the West, will undoubtedly provide entrepreneurship and capital needed for continued expansion.

This growth has not transformed Colorado into an industrial colossus and the contribution to the nation's industrial output is modest. The entire Rocky Mountain region creates only 2+ % of all value added by manufacturing with Colorado producing about one-third of that small proportion. Nevertheless, this manufacturing activity is more significant to the state's economy than our nationally renowned contributions to agriculture, recreation, and mining.

Table 2. LEADING MANUFACTURED
PRODUCTS-1978
Value Added – Millions of Dollars

Food and Kindred Products	$923.7
Machinery (excluding electric)	680.0
Fabricated Metal Products	417.4
Printing and Publishing	399.1
Primary Metal Industries	296.4
Rubber and Plastic Products	218.2

Table 3. MANUFACTURING – ROCKY
MOUNTAIN REGION
Value Added – Millions of Dollars

State	1978	1958
Colorado	$ 5,238	$ 762
Arizona	3,960	360
Utah	2,380	404
Idaho	1,844	246
New Mexico	795	206
Montana	851	186
Wyoming	426	65
	$15,494*	$2,229

*Represents 2.36% of U.S. total.

Manufacturing Percent of value added 1977

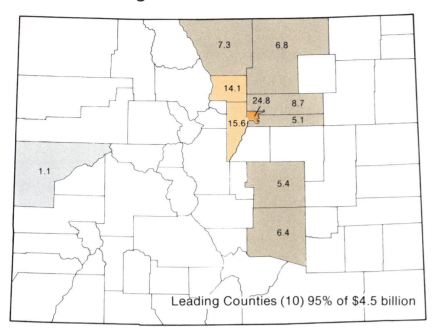

Leading Counties (10) 95% of $4.5 billion

Percent of Employees 1977

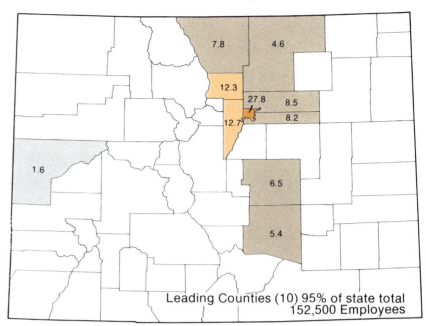

Leading Counties (10) 95% of state total
152,500 Employees

Percent of Payroll 1977

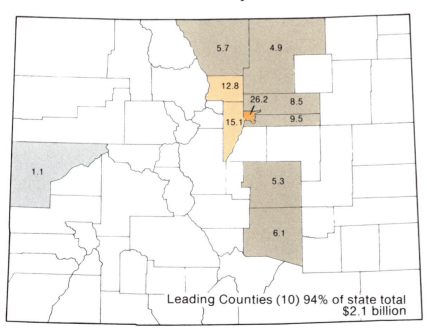

Leading Counties (10) 94% of state total
$2.1 billion

DISTRIBUTION
OF
MANUFACTURING
1977

Source: U.S. Census of Manufacturing, 1977

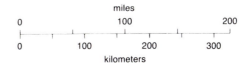

miles

0   100   200

0   100   200   300

kilometers

Recreation and Travel

AN OUTSTANDING combination of geographic circumstances has fostered a recreation industry that offers attractions of unusual variety and quality. From modest beginnings the industry has grown substantially so that it ranks with manufacturing, mining, and agriculture as a major employer and producer of wealth. The earliest available statistics indicate that about 1.3 million visitors spent approximately $38 million in each of the five years (1937–1941) prior to the onset of World War II. Forty years later (1981) 11.9 million vacationists spent $1.9 billion for lodging, food, drink, gasoline, retail, and other services.[1]

Although Colorado is far removed from major population centers, most vacationists and dollars spent are from out of state. Visitors and vacationing natives alike are lured by the major natural and cultural attractions, shown here as circles proportional to the number of visitors. The map clearly suggests that tourists are not solely interested in Colorado's natural "wonders" but are also concerned with human accomplishments as represented by the impressive cliff dwellings of Mesa Verde, by the unusually striking modern campus of the Air Force Academy or by the inspirational works and displays in a variety of museums.

The attractions map, however, sheds little light on other significant activities for which Colorado is justifiably renowned. The Southern Rockies, blessed with an abundance of powder snow, a long season, readily accessible slopes and excellent accommodations, have earned national and international acclaim as a skier's paradise. More than 30 areas with lift facilities and well-groomed slopes, plus scores of cross-country trails in the national forests, constitute a mecca for millions of in-state and out-of-state skiers. Most are attracted to the major resorts, especially those with a diverse mix of runs (trails) as suggested by their Vertical Transport Feet (V.T.F.).[2] A large V.T.F. suggests a great variety of skiing situations from ego-building runs for beginners to challenging trails for experts.

Seven major resorts, each selling more than 500,000 lift tickets per year, account for 68% of the downhill skier visits (Table 1). Geographically, a greater concentration occurs with 5 counties, attracting more than 80% of the skiers (Table 2).

Skiing, like other recreational activities, attracts participants from the urban centers of the Front Range corridor and the more populated segments of the United States. An estimated 35–40% of all skiers have origins in other states and countries. California, Texas, Illinois, New York and Michigan are major sources, especially their affluent suburbs. This influx of well-to-do urbanites contributes substantially to the economy of mountain counties and to Denver—the transfer point for most arrivals.

Hunting and fishing have a similar impact. Most individuals purchasing 1980 licenses

Table 1. AVERAGE ANNUAL SKIER VISITS
(1977–78 to 1981–82)

Vail	1,109,900
Winter Park	752,500
Snowmass	650,600
Keystone	599,600
Breckenridge	570,500
Copper Mountain	551,600
Steamboat	525,500
	4,760,300*

*68% of downhill skiers.

Table 2. SKIER VISITS BY COUNTY 1981–82

County	No. of Skiers	Areas
Summit	2,217,400	Keystone, Arapahoe, Copper Mtn., Breckenridge
Eagle	1,344,200	Vail, Beaver Creek
Pitkin	1,198,200	Snowmass, Aspen Highlands, Buttermilk, Aspen Mtn.
Grand	780,500	Winter Park, Ski Idlewild
Routt	613,500	Steamboat
	6,153,800*	

*80.7% of 7,622,300 skier visits to Colorado.

Table 3. HUNTING AND FISHING LICENSES – 1980 (PRELIMINARY)
(persons in thousands; dollars in millions)

	Resident		Non-resident		Total	
Hunting	380	$4.7	112	$12.0	492	$16.7
Fishing	430	3.4	218	2.0	648	4.5
	810	$8.1	330	$14.0	1140	$22.1

(71%) are residents, rather than non-residents (29%). The revenues gained from their sales have an inverse ratio with only 37% from residents and 63% from out-of-staters (Table 3).

A major and perhaps more characteristic aspect of the recreation industry involves the less affluent residents or non-residents who are attracted to our mountain and plateau landscapes within the national forests. In the 1980 fiscal year, approximately 22 million visitor days (including skiers) were reported, representing individuals from all walks of life who could choose from scores of either summer or winter activities for a modest expenditure of money or time. Hardy, athletic individuals are attracted to the "four-teeners" whose summit elevations exceed 14,000' and which offer daring or relatively easy ascents. Most people, however, pursue less strenuous activities and prefer to hike, camp, fish, photograph, or generally commune with nature.

Space limitations prevent adequate coverage of each recreational activity, for which there may be thousands or millions of enthusiasts. Together they have a significant impact on the state and local economies. New studies reflect all forms of travel to and within Colorado rather than just vacation and leisure travel and generally provide a better measure of the real worth and significance of the recreation industry. A recent

[1]Statistical sheet for Colorado Tourism prepared by the Colorado Office of Tourism Information and Services, Division of Commerce and Development, 1313 Sherman Street, Denver, Colorado 80203.

[2]Skiers who wish a minimum of waiting in lift lines will compare the two maps and choose those areas with a large V.T.F. and relatively few skiers.

Visitation to State Attractions

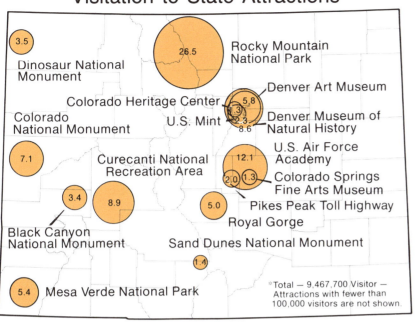

3.5
Dinosaur National Monument

26.5
Rocky Mountain National Park

Denver Art Museum
5.8
Colorado Heritage Center
1.3
U.S. Mint
2.3
Denver Museum of Natural History
8.6

Colorado National Monument

7.1

Curecanti National Recreation Area

12.1
U.S. Air Force Academy

2.0 1.3
Colorado Springs Fine Arts Museum

3.4

8.9

5.0
Pikes Peak Toll Highway

Royal Gorge

Black Canyon National Monument

Sand Dunes National Monument

1.4

5.4 Mesa Verde National Park

*Total — 9,467,700 Visitor — Attractions with fewer than 100,000 visitors are not shown.

Travel Expenditures

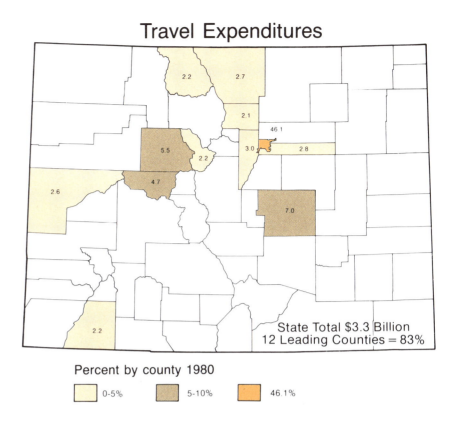

2.2   2.7

2.1

46.1

3.0   2.8

5.5   2.2

2.6   4.7

7.0

2.2

State Total $3.3 Billion
12 Leading Counties = 83%

Percent by county 1980

☐ 0-5%   ☐ 5-10%   ☐ 46.1%

Mountain Climbs

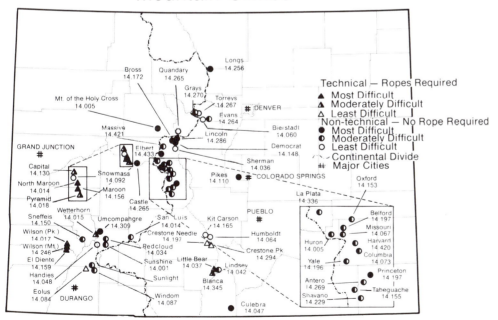

Bross 14.172
Quandary 14.265
Longs 14.256
Grays 14.270
Torreys 14.267
Mt. of the Holy Cross 14.005
Evans 14.264
DENVER
Bierstadt 14.060
Massive 14.421
Lincoln 14.286
GRAND JUNCTION #
Elbert 14.433
Democrat 14.148
Sherman 14.036
Capital 14.130
Snowmass 14.092
North Maroon 14.014
Maroon 14.156
Pikes 14.110
COLORADO SPRINGS
Pyramid 14.018
Castle 14.265
Oxford 14.153
Wetterhorn 14.015
La Plata 14.336
Sneffels 14.150
Umcompahgre 14.309
San Luis 14.014
Kit Carson 14.165
PUEBLO #
Belford 14.197
Wilson (Pk.) 14.017
Crestone Needle 14.197
Humboldt 14.064
Missouri 14.067
Wilson (Mt.) 14.246
Redcloud 14.034
Harvard 14.420
El Diente 14.159
Sunshine 14.001
Little Bear 14.037
Crestone Pk. 14.294
Huron 14.005
Columbia 14.073
Handies 14.048
Lindsey 14.042
Yale 14.196
Princeton 14.197
Eolus 14.084
Sunlight
Blanca 14.345
Antero 14.269
Taheguache 14.155
DURANGO
Windom 14.087
Shavano 14.229
Culebra 14.047

Technical — Ropes Required
▲ Most Difficult
▲ Moderately Difficult
△ Least Difficult
Non-technical — No Rope Required
● Most Difficult
◐ Moderately Difficult
○ Least Difficult
～ Continental Divide
Major Cities

TRAVEL AND RECREATION

1980

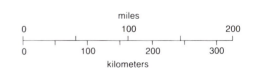

miles
0   100   200
0   100   200   300
kilometers

survey[3] indicates that during 1980 United States residents traveling away from home overnight or on day trips to places 100 miles or more spent $3.3 billion in Colorado, broken down as follows: transportation (40%); accommodations (16%); food (26%); entertainment and recreation (10%); and incidentals (8%). In per capita terms, travelers spent $1,159 for every resident.

At the local level, their expenditures contributed significantly to the general good. Twelve counties accounted for five-sixths of the $3.3 billion total, with Denver, Eagle, Pitkin, La Plata, Jackson and Summit receiving disproportionate shares in relation to their populations. El Paso County (Colorado Springs and Pikes Peak), long recognized as a tourist center, continues to attract a fair share of the tourist dollar but as in Arapahoe, Jefferson, Mesa, and Boulder Counties tourists contribute a relatively small share to the local economy.

[3]Colorado Travel and Tourism Statistics, 1980. Bureau Research Division, Graduate School of Business Administration, University of Colorado, Boulder, 1982, 49 pages.

Vertical Transport Feet 1981-82

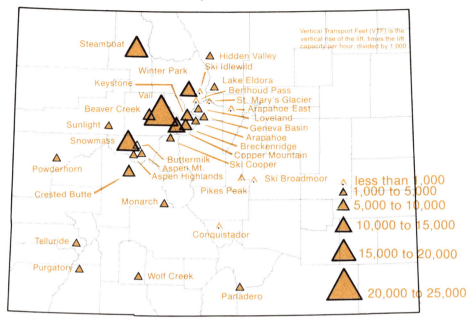

Ski Area Visits*

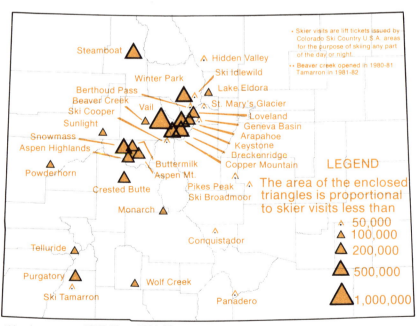

*Yearly average 1977-78 to 1981-82

Skier-Visits

1953-54 to 1981-82

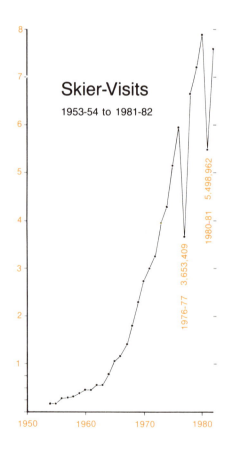

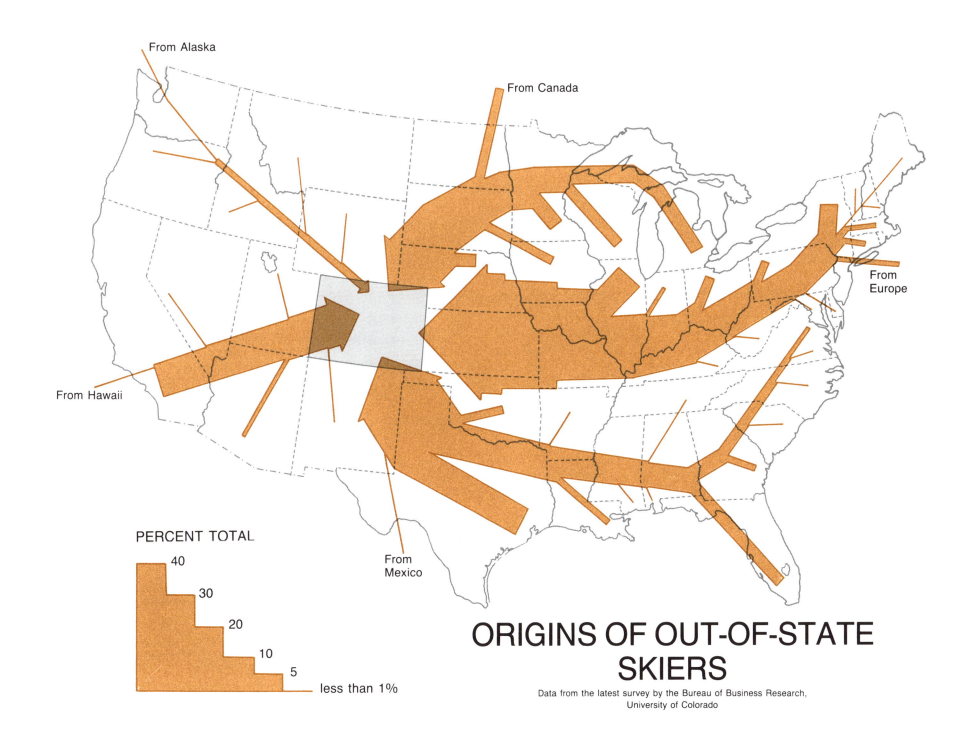

From Alaska

From Canada

From Europe

From Hawaii

From Mexico

PERCENT TOTAL

40

30

20

10

5

less than 1%

ORIGINS OF OUT-OF-STATE SKIERS

Data from the latest survey by the Bureau of Business Research,
University of Colorado

Transparation

THE TRANSPORTATION of people and commodities constitutes the "life blood" of modern American society. Anthropomorphic terminology for transport, such as "arteries" and "circulation," indicates just how vital that role is to the economic organism.

Colorado's transportation system benefits from historical development and from modern technology. The mining and prospecting heritage has left the state an intricate, finely engraved pattern of minor roads and trails that, considering the terrain and climate, provide surprising linkage and accessibility, a double-edged sword to those who cherish remoteness.

The same mining era produced the remarkable engineering achievements that brought the railroads, particularly the Denver and Rio Grande, high into the Rockies. The single western link to Utah from Pueblo and Denver dates from that period. However, the transcontinental lines skirted the confronting wall of mountains in Colorado with routes through northern New Mexico (Santa Fe) or southern Wyoming (Union Pacific). Following successive cattle and wheat frontiers, railroads pushed westward across the high plains from Nebraska and Kansas creating a ladder of parallel lines no more than 50 miles apart, all to terminate at Front Range cities (Atchison, Topeka, and Santa Fe [ATSF], Missouri Pacific, Kansas Pacific, Rock Island, Burlington).

Two products of postwar technology, the freeway and the jet airplane, have made Colorado a part of an important national transportation network. Interstate 70 links with I-25 to connect southern California to the mid-continental axis of Denver–Kansas City–St. Louis–Indianapolis–Pittsburgh–Baltimore. Connecting Billings, Montana, and El Paso, Texas, I-25 completes the north–south crosshair on Denver. Air traffic centers on Denver's Stapleton Airport, which received an average of 550 daily non-stop arrivals as of November 1, 1982. Stapleton handles nearly 25 million passengers each year, and ranks among the busiest airports in the nation.

The maps on the facing page indicate the distribution of traffic volumes. They literally show "lines of transportation," the lines in this case of varying width to represent the share of traffic carried. Each map uses a different method of measuring traffic share: average daily vehicle counts for highways, origin–destination by percentage of total passengers for air, and annual gross tons per mile for railroads.

Highways. The volume of daily traffic clearly highlights the Front Range urban complex and its interconnecting north–south freeway (I-25). Much of the route between Fort Collins and Colorado Springs exceeds 20,000 vehicles a day and urban traffic exceeds 30,000. The east–west interstates focus on Denver (I-76, I-70 from the east and I-70 westward). Of special note on the map are the somewhat surprising traffic intensities on some lesser routes: the Pueblo–La Junta connection, the Colorado Springs–Limon cutoff from I-70, the Glenwood Springs–Aspen–Independence Pass–Leadville route, the Montrose–Delta link along U.S. 50, and the extraordinarily high counts (15,000) for Craig's local traffic. Skier trips apparently play a role in the daily averages, to wit, the I-70 volume (10,000–15,000) over Loveland Pass, high local Aspen traffic, Berthoud Pass–Winter Park usage, and even the notable link between Gunnison and little Crested Butte.

Air Passengers. The diagonal transcontinental axis, northeast–southwest, that connects national population nodes, affects origin–destination patterns at the axial midpoint of Denver. Of the 25 million passengers, Los Angeles accounts for 5.6%, New York for 5.5%, which reflects the overall transcontinental pattern. Adding Chicago and Washington to New York's share brings the percentage to 12.3; to Los Angeles, the addition of Salt Lake City, San Francisco, Phoenix, and Las Vegas produces nearly 20%. Therefore, eight cities in all, three in the northeast, five in the southwest, account for nearly one-third of all passenger traffic at Denver. Outside this pronounced axis, Dallas–Fort Worth (4.8%) and Houston (4.2%) are important passenger links. Local service to Grand Junction and Albuquerque constitutes about 3% of the volume.

Railroads. The eye-catching tonnage of the transcontinental Union Pacific as it nips into northeastern Colorado (Julesburg) gives scale to the remainder of the Colorado rail system. The U.P. tonnage dwarfs by 12 times the main north–south line from Denver to Trinidad and the Burlington-Northern feeders to Denver from the northeast. Tonnage over Denver and Rio Grande trackage on the west slope is concentrated on two routes: the Arkansas Valley–Tennessee Pass and the Moffat Tunnel–North Park routes, joining at Dotsero to carry annually about 30 million tons per mile to the Utah border. Of passing note is the single line lacking linkage, the isolated narrow gauge relic now maintained for tourists between Durango and Silverton.

SELECTED REFERENCES

Colorado State Department of Highways, Division of Transportation Planning.
Stapleton International Airport, Engineering and Planning.

Highway Use

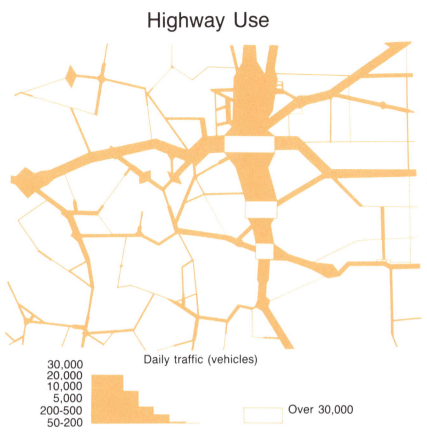

Daily traffic (vehicles)

30,000
20,000
10,000
5,000
200-500
50-200

Over 30,000

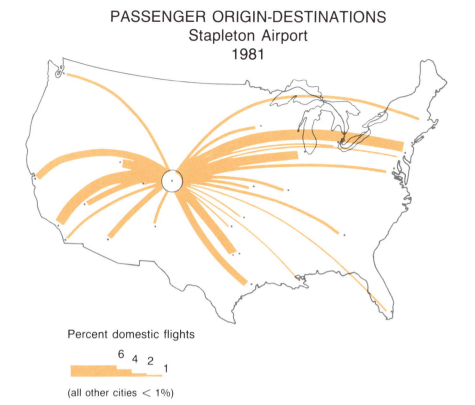

Percent domestic flights

6 4 2 1

(all other cities < 1%)

Railroad Volume

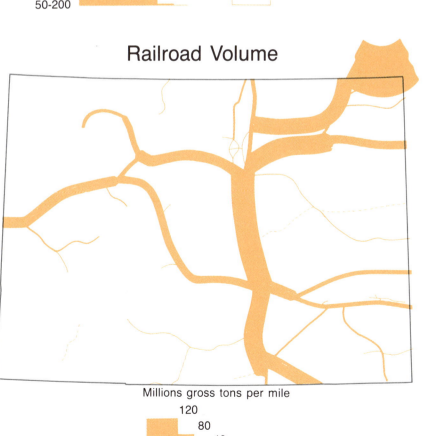

Millions gross tons per mile

120
80
40
1

TRANSPORTATION
FLOWS

Sources: Stapleton International Airport
State Department of Highways

miles

0   100   200

0   100   200   300

kilometers

Professional Service

PROFESSIONAL SERVICE may be defined loosely as the skilled service provided by people whose vocations require advanced training, usually beyond high school level. Traditional professions include medicine, law, and theology — the so-called "learned professions" — as well as engineering, architecture, science, education, and writing.

The concentration of professional people in any county may be expressed as the number of professionals per 1,000 county residents. Uneven distribution results from a number of interrelated factors: 1.) the population composition and distribution affects directly the demand for services. Particular age or income sectors of a population will create a market for a sensitive professional service. The sheer number of people will affect the number of professional people that can be supported and some sparsely populated counties may actually stand below a lower threshold of service. 2.) The economic character of a county or region will impact institutions and employment structures. A higher than normal number of architects, engineers, or lawyers could be expected in rapid growth areas. The economy will also influence the population, particularly its age and distribution, within a county and produce high or low levels of medical or educational service. 3.) Historic factors certainly play a role in professional concentrations. Often previous governmental decisions account for this, such as the selection of the state capitol, county seats, state hospitals, or scientific facilities. 4.) County boundaries and intervening transportation links may create better access to services in adjacent counties. It is easy to understand how county A could be served by professional service in adjacent county B. Statistically, county A would show a relatively low number of professionals, while county B would show a disproportionately high number. 5.) The nature of the profession itself should be considered a factor — most notably where mobility is characteristic of the service. Lawyers, for example, may provide their services through postal and telephone systems, and may appear in courtrooms or search records across the state, or nation. Thus, the choice of county residence may depend as well on amenities of the locality.

The maps on the facing page illustrate the varying concentrations of skilled people in the medical, legal, and educational professions. The information on actual number of professionals is converted to a ratio based on number per 1,000 population (1980) for each county. The average of these county ratios is referred to as the "County mean" (co. $\bar{x}$); the total number in the state as a ratio of total state population is the "state ratio."

Health Service. The county mean for health service employees is 23.4 per 1,000 population with the color distinction from gray representing the approximate breakpoint below or above the mean. Four counties stand considerably above the mean: Denver (46.2), Rio Grande (42.2), Pueblo (44.1), and Bent (103.8). The regional hospital in Las Animas, Bent County, functions as a referral center for Prowers and Baca Counties, and nearby Fort Lyons houses a federal veterans hospital which together total a substantial number (617) of medical personnel in a relatively low population agricultural county. Rio Grande's ratio is similarly inflated by the location of a nursing home for state veterans. Denver displays the typical high concentration of hospitals and medical care facilities of a large city and interstate regional service center. A number of surrounding counties, dependent on Denver's facilities, have relatively few health service employees. The remaining high ratio, Pueblo County, reflects the large number of nursing homes in the Pueblo area.

The low range counties, below 10 employees per 1,000, demonstrate a consistent pattern of low population, remote location, and mountainous terrain. San Juan (3.6) and Jackson (4.3) have the lowest ratios in the state. Summit County, only some 80 miles west of Denver, can hardly be called remote, but as a seasonal recreation county the resident population is small and unable to justify large medical care facilities.

Education. The county mean is 12.9 full-time teachers per 1,000 population. The counties above the mean have a typical dispersed rural population or a relatively large proportion of school-age children in the population. Kiowa is a county that accentuates the former condition, Costilla the latter.

Counties with a single large town or city tend to show ratios below the mean which probably reflects a little more efficient use of teachers (larger rooms with grade levels evenly distributed) and a population with relatively fewer children. Denver and the urbanized counties of the Front Range corridor display this tendency. Some of the mountain counties with a single large town in which most of the county population resides show a similar tendency. Pitkin County (Aspen) fits the stereotype and brings the teacher ratio to its nadir (6.09) with its high proportion of young adults and low share of school-age children in the population.

Legal Service. Three counties (Douglas, Kiowa, and Mineral) were without resident attorneys in 1983, although a business address for an attorney appeared in each county. This situation points to sparse populations unable to support a single full-time attorney and to the function of residence in an adjacent county. In all, 41 counties had fewer attorneys in residence than the county mean of 1.7 per 1,000. Once again, Pitkin County (Aspen) represents an extreme situation, this time with the highest ratio of lawyers to population (7.35) which indicates the peculiar economic and social characteristics of the county along with the amenities factor.

Health Employees

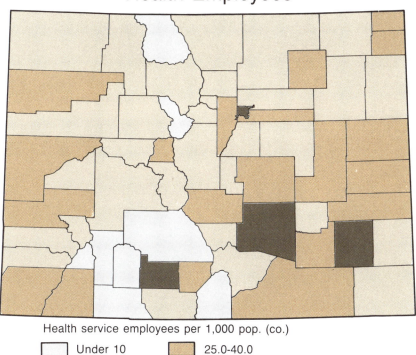

Health service employees per 1,000 pop. (co.)

Under 10	25.0-40.0
10.0-24.9	Over 40

Teachers

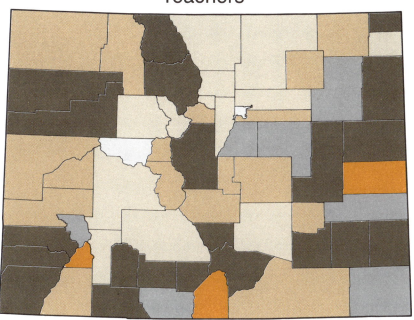

Certified full-time teachers per 1,000 pop. (co.)

Under 7	13.0-15.9
7.0-9.9	16.0-19.0
10.0-12.9	Over 19

Attorneys

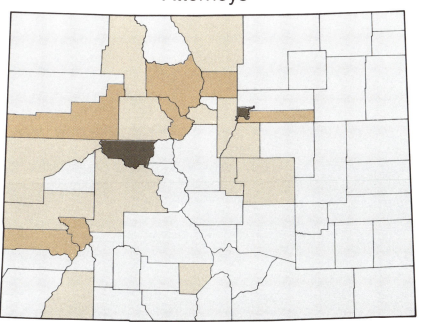

Active registered attorneys in residence (co.) per 1,000 pop. (co.)

0-1.69	3.40-5.09
1.70-3.39	Over 5.1

PROFESSIONAL SERVICES
County Distribution

Sources: U.S. Census of Population, 1980, Colorado Department of Education, 1982,
Colorado State Judicial Department, Colorado Supreme Court, 1983

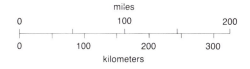

Environmental Quality

THE NATIONAL IMAGE of a healthful Colorado environment, albeit a bit tarnished by Denver's air pollution problem, remains essentially correct. The air quality over much of the state stands well above federal guidelines despite perplexing indications of acid precipitation in the Front Range, potential energy development, and the "Brown Cloud" of the metropolitan area. Water quality looks to be even better. The western two-thirds of Colorado records water qualities that can be matched in few states.

Air Quality. The quality of air depends on the amount of gaseous and particulate pollutants mixed with or suspended in the atmosphere. The gaseous pollutants, such as carbon monoxide and nitrogen oxides, are largely invisible, but may be highly toxic. The state of Colorado monitors continuously various gaseous pollutants at 15 urban stations in Fort Collins, Greeley, Boulder, Denver, Colorado Springs, Pueblo, and Grand Junction. Particulates, tiny particles suspended in the air, are monitored, usually every fourth day, at 62 sites across the state. From the monitoring stations peak counts and averages are developed that indicate air quality according to national standards.

The gaseous pollutants result largely from the burning of petroleum and coal. Carbon monoxide originates almost wholly from automobile traffic (in Denver, vehicular sources account for 94% of CO emissions). Amounts exceeding the one-hour standard (35 ppm) may impair heart functions in some individuals and were reached on 6 occasions (1981) at Broadway and Colfax in Denver; 48 violation days were recorded for the 8-hour standard (9 ppm). Nitrogen dioxide emanating from power plants and motor vehicles may corrode metals, damage plants, break down fabrics, and cause lung irritation. Similarly, ozone may adversely affect plant tissue and human respiration and results when hydrocarbons and oxides of nitrogen (NO$_x$) react with sunlight. Sulfur dioxide apparently poses no immediate threat to Colorado's air quality although only 3 stations (2 in Denver, 1 in Grand Junction) scarcely touch the potential emissions of typical stationary sources (power plants, smelters) across the state.

Total suspended particulates constitute the visible element in air pollution: the smoky haze in a mountain valley, the murky dust hanging over farmlands, or the urban smog of a Denver winter day. Particulates affect more than visibility; they also affect health. Eye irritation is the most obvious, but perhaps the most dangerous are the smallest particles (down to 0.1 micrometer) called respirable particulates, that interfere with oxygen production and cause shortness of breath, especially to those with sensitive respiratory diseases. The particulates themselves may be toxic or laden with toxic substances that penetrate the body's vital organs.

Two maps use 1981 data from the state department of health to plot total suspended particulates (TSP) over the state. The higher TSP annual averages (>80 μg) are shown in gray tone indicating counts exceeding the national standard (75 μg). The fifteen stations in the Denver metro area averaged 86 μg but the actual distribution within the area (see inset) depends greatly on winds, sources, and terrain which cause TSP ranges from low to extremely high annual geometric means, such as the downtown peak of 183 μg at Broadway and 21st which exceeds by nearly 3 times the national standard. A number of Western Slope communities recorded annual mean TSP over the minimum standard. These high counts may be attributed to local power plants and traffic, agricultural dust, and smoke from sawmill burners and resort fireplaces.

Water Quality. Amendments in 1972 to the Clean Water Act set a goal of making the nation's waters fishable and swimmable. Consequently, the draft report on Colorado's water quality (1982) by the Colorado Department of Health relies heavily on user criteria.

The map of the quality of surface waters represents a simplified version of state water quality standards. Pristine waters, streams much in the same condition as at the time of discovery, comprise the categories "High Quality, Class I, Class II" and are located exclusively in the often protected headwater highlands.

"Cold Water Aquatic Life, Class I" and "Warm Water Aquatic Life, Class I" together make up a very moderately or seasonally polluted group of streams that sustain naturally productive fisheries and typify most west slope stream segments. On the Eastern Slope, headwaters areas and some reservoirs qualify for this designation.

Lesser-quality symbols indicate a lumping together of all remaining classifications with "Recreation, Class 1" the highest of these. Lesser quality waters include a few short segments on the Western Slope (mining and irrigation areas) and lower Platte and Arkansas Rivers on the Eastern Slope. Amonia (NH$_3$), nitrates (NO$_3$), phosphates (PO$_4$), and fecal coliforms diminish user potential of these waters.

Salinity and mine drainage are special water problems associated with Colorado history. In past Colorado water agreements with downstream basin states, salinity standards have been established for Hoover, Parker, and Imperial Dams. Natural saline sources along the Colorado have been augmented by proximate consumptive use of water, primarily irrigation. The other problem, metal-mine drainage, dates back to the state's mining past. Its legacy of tailings, ponds, tunnels, and seepage may cause locally severe metallic contamination, but restoration of water quality is possible through control or clean-up at the point sources.

SELECTED REFERENCES

Hague, William S. and G. Carl Selnick, *Colorado Air Quality Data Report 1981*. Denver: Colorado Department of Health, 1982.

Water Quality Control Division, "Status of Water Quality in Colorado, 1982," Colorado Department of Health (draft copy).

Air Pollution: Particulates

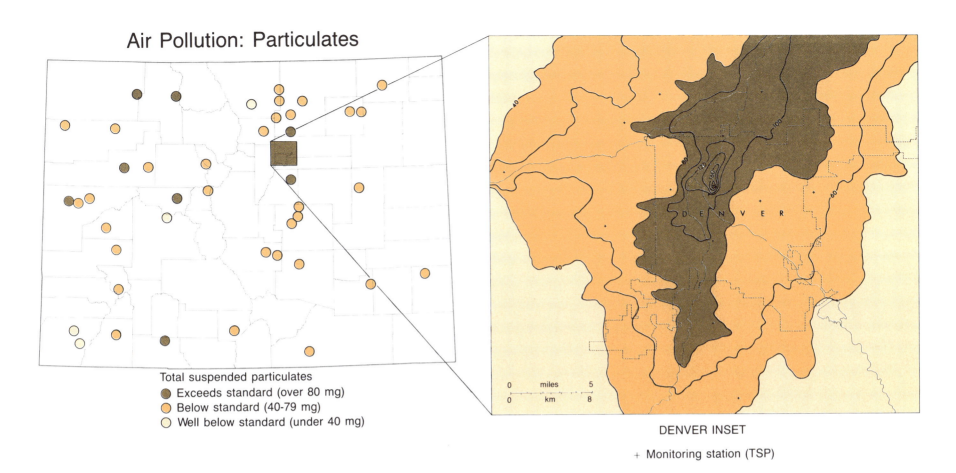

Total suspended particulates
- ● Exceeds standard (over 80 mg)
- ● Below standard (40-79 mg)
- ○ Well below standard (under 40 mg)

DENVER INSET

+ Monitoring station (TSP)

Water Quality

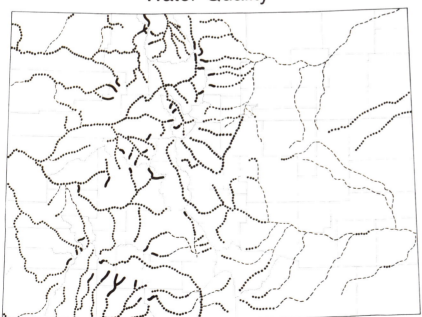

USER CLASSIFICATION
- ▬▬ Pristine waters
- ·········· Aquatic Life, Class I
- ----- Lesser quality

ENVIRONMENTAL QUALITY

Source: State Department of Health
(Air: 1981; Water: 1982)